A Sense of Style

BILL LUCAS

Oxford University Press   1989

Oxford University Press, Walton Street, Oxford OX2 6DP

Oxford New York Toronto
Delhi Bombay Calcutta Madras Karachi
Petaling Jaya Singapore Hong Kong Tokyo
Nairobi Dar es Salaam Cape Town
Melbourne Auckland

and associated companies in
Berlin Ibadan

Oxford is a trademark of Oxford University Press

ISBN 0 19 831166 4

Typesetting by Tradespools Ltd, Frome
Printed in Great Britain

ACKNOWLEDGEMENTS

The publishers and author would like to thank the following for their permission to
reproduce copyright material:

Ardea p.70, p.71 top and bottom;
John Cleare p.76, p.77, p.78 both, p.86, p.87 both;
Format (Jennie Matthews) p.23, p.24, (Joanne O'Brien) p.38 right, p.66, (Margaret
Murray) p.89 top, (Sunil Gupta) p.97 left, (Brenda Prince) p.97 right;
Sally and Richard Greenhill p.38 centre, p.57 left, centre right and right, p.67;
Impact p.91, p.124 top right;
Independent Newspapers Ltd p.47
Lafayette, Dublin, p.7
National Portrait Gallery p.108;
Christina Newman p.110 (both)
Network (Mike Abrahams) centre left;
Oxford and County Newspapers p.48;
Paramount Pictures p.120;
Popperfoto p.16, p.17, p.30, p.31, p.32 left, p.122, p.124 centre top, bottom right;
John Powell p.65 (all)
Sunday Times (Gugliemo Galven) p.50, (Tim O'Sullivan) p.52, (Jeremy Young) p.53;
Topham Picture Library p.13, p.80, p.81, p.124 top left, centre left, bottom left,
centre bottom;
Simon Warner p.38 bottom, p.85 bottom, p.89 bottom, p.93, p.94.

Contents

How to use this book

1 Use the Contents page to help you find the area of your choice.

2 Each unit:
- has plenty of pieces for you to read,
- contains discussion activities to improve your oral work,
- offers a variety of assignments suitable for GCSE English coursework,
- allows you to build up an overall understanding of a particular style of writing.

3 At the end of each unit:

- There is a special feature in which a longer, more detailed coursework assignment is suggested.

Example from page 54.

> On these pages are various articles and information about certain skills to enable you to research and then produce an extended piece of work called *Living in the 1990s*.

- There is a list of key words and key techniques.

Example from page 17.

Key words

autobiographical
incidents feelings
memories experiences
challenges
development details
remember select
material personal

4 Use the assignment index on page 127 to help you choose suitable areas and to give you an idea of what is involved in a particular piece of work.

Example from page 127.

1	My first love	Autobiography
2	Two chapters of an autobiography	Autobiography
3*	Going away to London	Opinion essay
4	How to ...	Guide for younger children

Some suggestions for producing coursework

1 All English GCSE exams encourage you to develop pieces of writing over a period of time. They demand a great variety of styles of writing, including those presented in this book.

You are likely to produce your best work when you are clear *who* you are writing for and when the assignment is as genuine and realistic as possible. For this reason there will be several occasions when you will want to adapt suggestions in the book to make them particularly relevant to yourself.

2 Just as a published writer produces various drafts before writing the final book, so you may need to go through different stages before writing a final version. Here are some easily-adapted methods to follow.

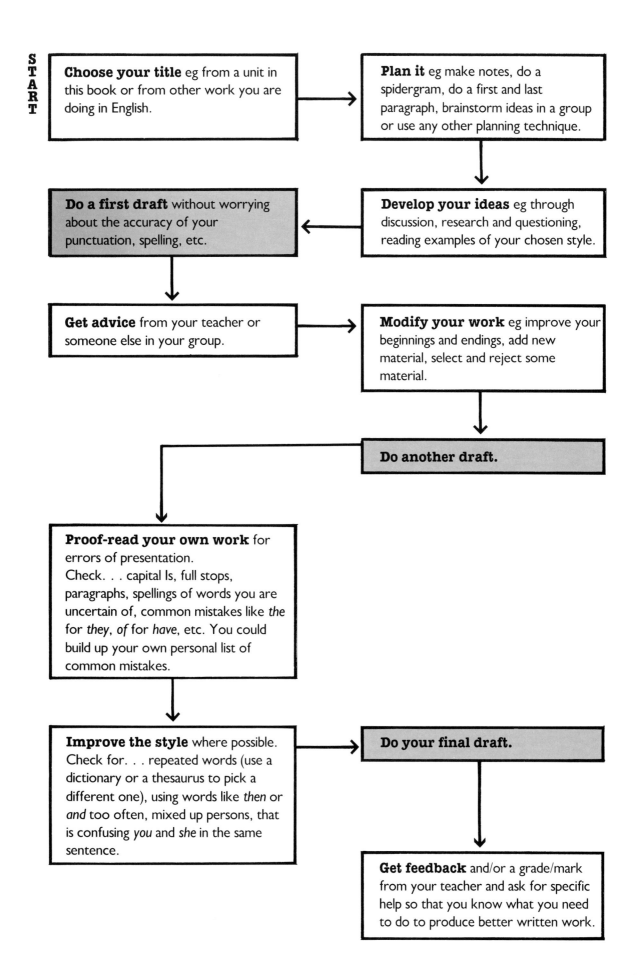

START

Choose your title eg from a unit in this book or from other work you are doing in English.

Plan it eg make notes, do a spidergram, do a first and last paragraph, brainstorm ideas in a group or use any other planning technique.

Do a first draft without worrying about the accuracy of your punctuation, spelling, etc.

Develop your ideas eg through discussion, research and questioning, reading examples of your chosen style.

Get advice from your teacher or someone else in your group.

Modify your work eg improve your beginnings and endings, add new material, select and reject some material.

Do another draft.

Proof-read your own work for errors of presentation.
Check. . . capital Is, full stops, paragraphs, spellings of words you are uncertain of, common mistakes like *the* for *they*, *of* for *have*, etc. You could build up your own personal list of common mistakes.

Improve the style where possible. Check for. . . repeated words (use a dictionary or a thesaurus to pick a different one), using words like *then* or *and* too often, mixed up persons, that is confusing *you* and *she* in the same sentence.

Do your final draft.

Get feedback and/or a grade/mark from your teacher and ask for specific help so that you know what you need to do to produce better written work.

UNIT I *Autobiography*

Talking and writing about your life are important ways of helping you to understand yourself.

Read these two pieces of autobiographical writing.

Is that it?

Sometimes I would bunk out of study and go down to see Cully. He had a big tree in front of his house where you could play Tarzan and Boy, or Plarzan and Lad, as we called it. But Cully always got to be Plarzan because he was stronger. When it was time for tea Cully would never ask me in. I don't know why. I'd have to wait outside on the steps and then it would grow dark but I couldn't go home because study didn't finish till eight and therefore I couldn't appear in the house till eight-thirty for fear of my skiving being discovered. If I had any money, I would go down to the fish shop in Blackrock and get smoked cod and chips. It cost two shillings.

Two shillings was a lot, but I had the cash from my school fees. Every week before he went on his travels around Ireland my father would give me my school fees money in an envelope. It was nice to have some money so I opened the envelope myself instead of handing it in to the school office. It was a few pounds. You could buy cream buns from The Nook or use it to go to the pictures on Saturday afternoon at the Adelphi. No one seemed to mind. But then, at the end of that term, a bill came. He rang the school without telling me.

'Good morning, Father Stanley,' said the boys in chorus. He did not enter the class during lessons except for some serious reason.

'Robert Geldof. Will you please leave the classroom?'

Everyone looked at me. I moved my books to the corner of my desk and straightened my pencil – half wanting to impress the Dean with my neatness, half wanting to put off, even if only for a few seconds, the awful moment when I would discover why he wanted me. I had no idea. But I felt in my stomach that it must be bad.

I stood in the corridor in silence as the story of my wrong-doing was recounted. Somehow from his lips the whole thing sounded far worse than it had ever seemed to me. '. . . It is not simply the amount, though that is grave of itself; your father is by no means a wealthy man, he makes sacrifices to send you here. He will now have to find the amount which you owe to the school. But it is more than that. It is the deceit and dishonesty it embodied. Such behaviour is sinful. Your father and I have talked about the whole matter. He is going to beat you and so am I.'

Father Stanley had what the boys called a 'biffer'. The word was a joke, but the implement was not. A thick, flexible rubber strap, it hurt unbearably. I was outraged and shamed by this terrible injustice. But what happened at home was much worse. There was no one to plead for me. I was utterly alone. On the bus home, in panic, I prayed to my mother. I was in pain from the beating at school and in terror of what lay ahead.

First there was the silence and the sobbing.

'Why did you do it?' Lynn asked me. Lynn was supposed to be my friend.

'I don't know. It didn't seem that important. I'm sorry.'

'Don't you know that since Mammy died the house has had to run on trust while Daddy is away all week? We are all on our honour to behave ourselves,' said Cleo. Cleo was a grown-up, more than twenty now, but she was only my sister. Why should she be allowed to speak to me like this? 'I'm on my honour to be in by ten o'clock every night and I don't break the trust. Lynn is on her honour to do her schoolwork for her Intermediates and she doesn't break the trust. But you, you can't even be trusted to take in your dinner money. Why did you do it?'

'I don't know. I'm sorry, I'll pay it back.'

'Go upstairs, Robert,' said my father.

There was a sofa in the room where he hit me. He spoke to me first. 'This will hurt me more than it hurts you.' He actually said that. It did not seem real, it was like some schoolboy novel. What was most horrible was that he had got a bamboo cane to hit me with. Had he gone out and bought it? The cold-blooded calculation of that simple act is the thing that still bothers me. He had decided to inflict as much pain as he could. He had thought about that as he chose it: 'No, that one won't be as painful as this cane.'

'I am going to hit you six times.' His voice was cold. 'You are never going to do this again. Hold on to the back of the sofa and bend over.'

'No, Da. Please don't hit me. I'll be good now.' I still didn't really grasp what had been so bad. I ran around the sofa.

'Come back.'

I went to the sofa and held fast to it. My knuckles were white with the gripping, but they did not seem like my own. I felt as though I was watching someone else's hands. The cane swished and a hot line of pain cut across my buttocks. It burned like the pain you got when your hand brushed by accident against the kitchen stove. I howled, but I did not move. The second would be easier, I told myself. But it wasn't, it was a hurt on top of the hurt. My whole body was now entirely concentrated in those few inches of flesh. The third set my entire being into a contortion of agony. I screamed and ran away.

'Come back.'

'No.'

'Please, Da. Please, no more, please.'

He chased me around the room, grabbed me and hit out again and again. I could not believe he would do this. Then, at the end, the bastard tried to hug me. How dare he salve his own pathetic conscience with that act of hypocrisy? If you're going to hurt someone, hurt them, but don't pretend it's love. That's perversion. I was filled with disgust and I hated him. The hurt, the rage, the shame and the bewilderment were too deep. From that day on, my father and I were at loggerheads. He would pay.

by *Bob Geldof*

My life

Why I am writing this story about my life is because my life is a bad and a good life. Well, where shall I start now? I will start when I was a little boy, when I was in Morocco. I come from Morocco. I lived in Larache. It is a very good town. I lived in a house in a street called Cospa. Well it was great over there, a wonderful place. I lived there with my mum and my father, very happy. And what I mean by happy is I was with my mum and my father.

My father worked with a Spanish man in a restaurant and my mum was a housewife. Now I'm talking about the good things, happy days and happy minutes, happy seconds as well. We always went out on Friday to the market and sometimes to the seaside and sometimes walked around the town. And on Sundays we went to see our grandma and grandpa. When I was about ten years old I was still happy, of course. But then my father thought of going abroad, to Spain or England and he was asking for information.

My mother and his mother said, 'You can't go and leave us on our own,' and my mother said, 'We can never enjoy our lives.' My father said, 'We will be happy after and we will have more money. We can't go on here.' He got his passport. That took about six months, but my father was lucky because people have waited ages for a passport. My father wanted to go to England. My father was happy and we were happy and not very happy because we were going to miss him, and he was going to live on his own and it is a very different country.

He went to Tangiers to get a ticket with my mother. And the time was going so fast. And it seemed to us horrible because we had never been without the big man.

It was his last night in Morocco. He was very sad and he was talking to my mother, and he said, 'Look after the children.' And my mother said to him, 'Do you have to go?' He said, 'We can't just stay here with our lives going fast.'

The morning came, and what a morning it was – not as bright as the other days, so dark. We woke up early to go with our father to Tangiers. He was going to catch a ship and then a train to Scotland.

He caught a coach to Tangiers and it was good going on the coach, but it would have been much better if we were all going for a holiday. But it had to come.

We got off the coach in Tangiers and it was the afternoon about three o'clock. The boat was leaving at four o'clock. We all carried the bags and my father carried the suitcase. My father's face was white and he didn't know what to do next.

He started to kiss us and he was crying like a little boy. I have never seen my father crying like that. We were all crying. And they were calling the people to go to their places on the boat, but we wouldn't let our father go. It seemed a horrible day.

Then our father went on the ship and he went on the deck. He got out his handkerchief and started waving with it. The ship left and he was still waving. We were all crying.

My mother said to me, 'Come son, he will come back some day,' and I told that to my little brothers. We went to the coach station to catch the coach. We got on the coach and left Tangiers. It was horrible going on the coach, all silent, none of us were talking.

We went home. My mother was still crying. My grandma came to our house and she was crying as well. The day passed, and thank God it did.

The next morning was a morning without a father. He was still travelling because it would take him about five days to get to Scotland.

by *Mohammed Elbaja*

I In groups, make a list of everything about the two extracts which is similar. Your list could refer to what happened or the way it is described. The lines which follow are included to give you some ideas.

'Sometimes *I* would bunk out of study and go down to see Cully . . .'
'*I* lived in a house in a street called Cospa . . .'

'Two shillings *was* a lot . . . it *was* nice . . . He *rang* the School . . .'
'I *was* with my mum and my father . . . we *went* to see our grandma . . . He *got* his passport.'

'My knuckles were white with the gripping . . .'
'My father's face was white and he didn't know what to do next . . .'

'The hurt, the rage and the bewilderment were too deep . . .'
'It was horrible going on the coach, all silent, none of us were talking.'

2 Mohammed Elbaja was still at school when he wrote his autobiography; Bob Geldof looks back to his schooldays. Both writers write about strong feelings. In groups talk about how far you understand or sympathize with these feelings.

3 Talk about why you think these incidents were important to the writers and what effects they had on them.

Often it is first experiences which provide powerful memories in any autobiography.

First experiences

In this unpublished piece Sue, a blind girl, describes her first lesson in a Sunshine Home.

I spent a long time in the cloakroom trying to do up my buttons. Miss Barratt and Nurse Edna came in with the younger children so I asked Nurse Edna if she'd help me, but Miss Barratt told her to let me do it myself. I sat on the cloakroom bench and started to cry because I didn't like Miss Barratt's tone of voice. I heard Miss Barratt walk away. I knew it was her because of her heavy footsteps. Then I heard a kind voice say 'What's the matter dear? Don't you feel well?' It was Nurse Edna. I told her I couldn't do my buttons up and that I didn't like Miss Barratt because she was unkind. She did them up for me and said 'I'll teach you to do your buttons. Miss Barratt isn't unkind. She just likes you to try.'

Back in the classroom the other children were given various jobs to do, such as writing, the sorting-tray and putting pegs in a board. I was told to find a seat and wait for the teacher. While I was waiting I wondered what 'the sorting-tray' was and I made up my mind to ask her when she came to me. She came over and sat beside me and tipped some money on to the table and asked me to feel each coin and tell her what it was. When I'd finished I asked her what the sorting-tray was and she told me that she put little objects in a large tray with four compartments and we were expected to feel where each object was supposed to go. The same thing was done with the money and I was given a tray and told to put the right coin in the right compartment. Every now and again I heard a child say they'd finished and Miss Patterson would tell them to bring the work to her and I was still sorting the money. After a while she came over to see how I was getting on. I stopped when I felt her standing beside me. I heard her take a coin out. She handed it to me, saying, 'Feel that and tell me what it is.' It had a smooth edge: it was a penny. She told me to feel where it should go. Then she told me I'd put it in with the halfpennies. She took all the money out and put it back in her purse. She then told me that I was going to practise sorting money every day for a week until I could do it properly.

After a couple of weeks, Sue makes a breakthrough.

Later Nan came to collect me and I told her I was learning to read.* She was pleased to hear that but she wasn't pleased to hear I still couldn't do my buttons. All that weekend mum tried to get me to do them. I had learned to undo them but I couldn't do them up. Poor mum was very upset when she tried to teach me because I kept trying to pull them off.

*She is learning to read braille.

It was one morning when we were all getting ready to go into the grounds when I suddenly said 'Miss Patterson, look I've done my buttons up.' She undid them and asked me to show her again. Then she called Miss Barratt:

'Susan can do her buttons now.' Then she kissed me and told me I was a good girl and I could hear that there were tears in her voice. I felt very pleased with myself and waited to hear Miss Barratt's comments but she neither commented nor kissed me.

When mum came home from work, she asked me how I'd been behaving and was Miss Patterson pleased with my work. I told her that I had a surprise for her but before I went to get my coat to show her, I told her what new lessons I had learned. When mum and I had finished talking, I put my coat back on and said, 'Mum watch this.' I did my buttons up and undid them. 'Good girl,' she said, kissing me. Aunt Shirley came and took me shopping and to see her friend and we had a lovely time chatting and laughing. It was a weekend to remember for I dressed myself completely.

1 What are the first experiences that Sue is describing?

2 What other areas of ordinary 'sighted' life would be particularly challenging for a blind person? Agree a list of five of these. Explain the particular difficulties each would present.

3 What are the early challenges or developments that you remember? In your group, brainstorm them and then choose three to discuss?

4 Agree a title for this extract which best sums up what you consider to be its main point. Compare your title with those of other groups.

Descriptions of first experiences of love are often included in autobiographical writing.

First experiences of love

Read this account of it written by a fourteen-year-old school student.

My first love

'Come on, run!' said Tony. 'Run, we'll miss the bus.'

'Hang on I'm coming.'

It was just after sports' day in the second year. I was in no fit state to sprint for the bus as I had just run the fifteen hundred metres. I was with a boy called Tony Pariola who was a coloured boy. He was a good friend and he needed to be for what was in store for us.

We got on the bus at Blackheath village. We made our way to the top deck of the bus where we were unexpectedly greeted by two girls. One was about thirteen, with blond hair and fairly white complexion. She was, as we later found out, Vivien Brown. The other was fifteen with blondy-brown coloured hair. She had lovely eyes and a cool sun-tanned face. She was Amanda Davis.

We started talking to them. I felt very nervous and shy because it was obvious that Amanda had her eye on me. I couldn't believe it. She was beautiful and she wanted me.

Vivien did all the talking.

'What's your name?' she said to me.

'Oh, err . . .'

'Richard,' Tony butted in. This made me look a bit of a fool. Amanda just kept staring at me with those lovely blue eyes of hers. I felt really uncomfortable as I hadn't had much experience with girls in the past. No one said much on that journey. Finally it was time to get off the bus. I went down the stairs thinking that it had been just another wasted opportunity when Tony ran down after me.

'Rich, she asked me if you want to go out with her; she really fancies you.' This was a bit of an indignity as it is traditionally the boy's task to make the first move.

'Err, I'll tell her tomorrow,' I said unsure of what I was saying.

The next day after school I was walking to the bus-stop with Tony.

'I'm telling you Rich, she badly fancies you. Oh, by the way I told her you said yes.'

'Oh thanks Tony,' I said sarcastically, even though inside I was quite relieved that that little matter was sorted out.

On the bus I sat next to her with my arm around her, feeling a bit of a fool. Tony and Vivien were chatting away like old friends and all I could manage was a couple of words in the whole journey. I didn't feel right.

We parted company at my bus-stop with a kiss, and the rest, and said goodbye.

The next day on the bus I did a bit more talking.

'How old are you?' I said to Amanda.

'Fifteen nearly sixteen.'

'Oh dear,' I thought, as I was only thirteen.

'How old are you?' she said.

'Fifteen,' Tony butted in, I was glad he said it as I wouldn't have been able to without looking obviously guilty. I could see that Amanda didn't really believe me but didn't care.

The next day was one of the most depressing of my life. A boy called Mark Picton, who was a St Austin's fifth former, got on the bus. Amanda and Vivien weren't there. He started telling me and Tony what type of girl Amanda was and it wasn't the type that thirteen-year-old Catholic boys should mix with. I also heard that she was two-timing me with another boy who was sixteen. Suddenly I felt very small, in fact, I nearly fell through a crack in the floor.

The next day I felt so depressed when I was with Amanda. I knew it was too good to last. She was such a beautiful girl, it seemed such a waste. That night I told Vivien that I didn't want to know Amanda any more.

I thought it was the biggest mistake in my life later on. About a week later I found out that what the fifth former from St Austin's had told me was a pack of lies. I also heard that she was now going out with him. I was angry and heart-broken and I'll never forget that summer of eighty-three for being such a gullible fool. I still think of that girl now and what could have happened if I hadn't been tricked.

by *Andrew Calman*

In pairs, talk about your own experiences of love or try to put them straight on to paper.

Assignment 1

Write a section for your own autobiography called *My First Love*. Concentrate on some of these features:

how you were feeling,
what your face revealed of what you were feeling,
the setting,
some of the dialogue from your scene. (Think of some of the lines used on first dates.)

History and geography

Read these two pieces of writing. The first piece has been published as an autobiography, *London smog* was written by an adult remembering her childhood and has not been published before.

A child in the forest

Coal was no problem, except for the miners too old or too ill to work, for every working miner had an allowance of twelve hundredweight a month. The wonders of gas and electricity we only knew of secondhand from girls on holiday from service. Candles and paraffin lamps lit us up.

Often our home couldn't afford paraffin – or even, on occasion, a candle. Many's the time I've been sent around trying to borrow 'a stump o' candle'. Come to that, I was often sent for 'a pinch o' tay', 'a lick o' marge', 'a screw o' sugar', 'a sliver o' soap', or 'a snowl o' bread'. No one was ever optimistic enough to try to borrow money.

Each cottage garden was fenced with a dry-stone wall to keep out the sheep and pigs. Old iron bedsteads mostly served as garden gates. Any cottager who could afford it kept a pig; some were spare-time sheep-badgers, taking advantage of an ancient right to graze their sheep in certain areas of the surrounding forest. We children loved watching the dipping, shearing, and marking rituals, but only a hardy few could bear to watch the slaughter of a pig.

Pigs were regarded practically as neighbours. They had their own little stone dwellings alongside the cottages, and were christened with pretty names like Rosie, Sukey, or Ginny. Knots of men leaned over the pigs' gates to drool over the plump, succulent charmers in the pens. A weary, coal-grimed man would stop for a slap and tickle with the pig before going indoors from work, answering her welcoming squeals and grunts with his own brand of piggy endearments. Shopkeepers would often refuse credit for family groceries, yet supply bran on tick for the pig; then they could claim half the pig at killing.

by *Winifred Foley*

How does the mention of these details – coal, candles, pigs, credit – give us a fuller picture of rural life in the past. When do you think the author is writing about? What clues tell you this?

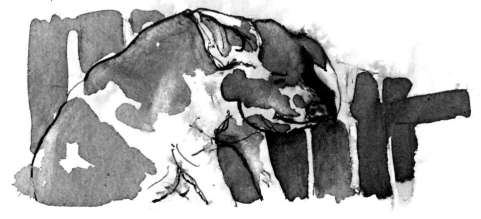

London smog

One of the greatest health hazards at this time was the polluted air.

In December 1952 the London area was covered in smog for four consecutive days. Nearly five thousand people died as a result. Many of us were ignorant of the danger of inhaling air polluted by smog, which was a mixture of smoke and fog. Much of the smoke came from factory chimneys, but smoke from domestic coal fires contributed greatly to the formation of smog. In London after the war many prefabs were built very quickly in order to meet the housing shortage. These small dwellings had low roofs, and smoke emitting from their chimneys did not rise much above ground level, especially on a still day. At times, a pall of smoke would hang over a prefab site when the surrounding area was clear. Even a wind would merely spread the smog, not disperse it.

My husband remembers trying to watch a football match at Charlton's Valley Club. During the first half of the game the visibility was quite good. A cloud of smog in the distance, however, gradually crept nearer, and completely blotted out the second half of the game!

What picture of city life in the 1950s does this create? Pick out the details which add to this.

Other features

On the following pages some other features of autobiographical writing are illustrated:

- using dialogue effectively
- remembering and then bringing memories alive
- using descriptions to bring writing alive
- linking past events with what is happening at the time

Read these pieces of writing. List the techniques you think are being used in each one.

1

'If thee doosn't go to sleep Feyther Christmas wunt come at all,' she scolded me.

'I can't,' I wailed, 'thee'lt' a' to 'it I over the yud wi' the coal 'ammer.'

I banged my obstinate head into the bolster. 'Go to sleep, you silly little bitch,' I told myself crossly.

It was my excited little brother who poked *me* awake in the morning. 'Look – Feyther Christmas a' brought I a tin whistle, a orange, a bag o' marbles an' some sweets.'

I sat bolt upright, like a Jack-in-the-Box. My doll, my doll! Had Father Christmas brought my doll?

At the bottom of my piece of the bed was propped the ugliest apology for a doll one could ever hope not to see.

It looked for all the world like an old, darned, black woollen stocking, lumpily stuffed, with a bit of old ribbon tied tightly round the foot to form its head. The eyes were two odd-sized buttons, and it grimaced from ear to ear with a red woollen gash of a mouth.

After all that cajoling up the chimney, after all the notes I'd written, fancy him bringing me a thing like that! He must think me a horrible little girl to treat me so, but I couldn't be that horrible! Mam came in, looking a bit anxious, but she said, bright enough, 'Well then, Feyther Christmas didn't forget. 'Im did bring a doll for you.'

'Yes, an' 'im can 'ave the bugger back.'

Mother looked crestfallen. 'It won't break, like one o' they china dolls.'

'It's ugly, an' boss-eyed, an' got no 'air, and 'ow would you like it if the angels sent you a babby as ugly as *that*?'

Then I pulled the quilt over my head, to show I had cut myself off from the season of goodwill, and everyone concerned with it.

But Mam hadn't. After a bit she came back and sat on the bed. She didn't say anything, and my curiosity soon overcame me enough to have a peep at what she was up to.

From *A Child in the Forest*
by *Winifred Foley*

2 My life! There has been nearly fifteen years of it so far. Remembering some clearly and other things vaguely. The first thing I can remember is having a little table and chair when I was about two or three years old. I had this table when I was living in Stratford. I was living in a flat and the strangest thing I can remember is the large kitchen with a two-level floor. That's the only thing I can remember about that time of my life. The next five years of my life were, I think, the most interesting years.

From Rare Bengal Tiger by Mayank Patel

4 I remember that when I was around three years old, I was asleep in my parents' bed. My father was at work, my mother was out shopping and Ali was busy with the housework. Avani, my sister, who is younger than me, was asleep in her cot. I woke up feeling very thirsty. I looked around the bed for my bottle but to my dismay could not find it. I noticed a bottle on the floor with transparent liquid inside it. I jumped out of the large bed and walked towards the bottle. I drank it and later felt a burning pain inside my stomach. That moment my mother walked in and I passed out. In later life I was told that the paraffin had been pumped out of my stomach by means of tubes and I was lucky to be alive.

From Home to Home by John Hawkridge

3 The house where I was born, in April 1904, was steep and chilly. It stood in the Old Brompton Road, in South Kensington, and the horse-drawn traffic, vans, cabs and carriages roared and clattered along outside, noisier even, I seem to remember, than the lorries and cars so soon to take their place. In winter the bedrooms and bathrooms were particularly cold. I hated the tepid baths and the icy, linoleum-covered floors which surrounded them; the occasional hipbath, allowed only when I was ill, and taken in front of the nursery fire, with a big towel being warmed on the high fender, was a luxury to which I greatly looked forward.

Winter too brought the fogs, impenetrably thick. I would find my way home holding one hand in front of me for fear of colliding with someone coming in the opposite direction, while with the other I tapped along the railings with a stick.

From An Actor and his Time by John Gielgud

5 The June grass, amongst which I stood, was taller than I was, and I wept. I had never been so close to grass before. It towered above me and all around me, each blade tattooed with tiger-skins of sunlight. It was knife-edged, dark, and a wicked green, thick as a forest and alive with grasshoppers that chirped and chattered and leapt through the air like monkeys.

I was lost and didn't know where to move. A tropic heat oozed up from the ground, rank with sharp odours of roots and nettles. Snow-clouds of elder-blossom banked in the sky, showering upon me the fumes and flakes of their sweet and giddy suffocation. High overhead ran frenzied larks, screaming, as though the sky were tearing apart.

From Cider with Rosie by Laurie Lee

Some questions to help your understanding of these can be found on page 17.

On these pages are various ideas to help you write two chapters for your own autobiography.

▼ Assignment 2 · A first chapter

Read what Roald Dahl places at the beginning of his autobiography, *Boy*.

An autobiography is a book a person writes about his or her own life and it is usually full of all sorts of boring details.

This is not an autobiography. I would never write a history of myself. On the other hand, throughout my young days at school and just afterwards a number of things happened to me that I have never forgotten.

None of these things is important, but each of them made such a tremendous impression on me that I have never been able to get them out of my mind. Each of them, even after a lapse of fifty and sometimes sixty years, has remained seared on my memory.

I didn't have to search for any of them. All I had to do was skim them off the top of my consciousness and write them down.

Some are funny. Some are painful. Some are unpleasant. I suppose that is why I have always remembered them so vividly. All are true.

Questionnaire

Use this questionnaire to help you 'skim' some things off 'the top of' your 'consciousness'.

1 What are the first names you remember?

2 What was your first school like?

3 Which members of your family do you have early memories of?

4 What was your bedroom like. . .size? colour? smell?

5 Did you always live in the same house?

Techniques

- Talk about some of your memories.
- Try and avoid any details which don't add to your story.
- Select carefully and don't worry if you have several false starts.
- Use some of the techniques in this unit.
- Decide who you are writing for.

An important chapter

No one can tell you which of all your experiences it is important to select. For blind Sue it was her buttons; for you it may be something completely different. For Lynne Jones it was her decision to be part of the blockade.

Keeping the peace

'Isn't this getting a little ridiculous?' the policeman asked. 'How many more of you want to get arrested?' Ridiculous to you perhaps, I thought, to me it seems like the most sensible thing I've ever done in my life.

'We don't want to get arrested. That's not why we're here. We're blocking all the entrances to this camp for 24 hours to show we intend to close it down, because we object to what's going on in there. If you choose to arrest us, that is your affair.'

It was 2.00 pm on a Monday afternoon in March, the first warm day of the year. We stood on a quiet country road, Newbury Church just visible over the horizon, the hedges and trees just touched by a green mist, a lark singing, high and clear, peace. For the third time that afternoon women lay down head to toe to fill a gap in the wire fence enclosing the base . . .

I'd been nervous about the blockade. We'd talked about it for weeks. It was to follow on from a festival to celebrate the Spring Equinox. While plans for the festival had gone smoothly ahead, because of concern over the threatened eviction we'd done little to prepare for the blockade. So I had arrived at the camp two days previously with a sick feeling in my stomach that we were heading for disaster. 'Don't worry Lynne,' Shushu had smiled, patting my shoulder, 'We're very organised.' And indeed they had been. One group of women had written a small practical briefing, outlining how the blockade would proceed, what to do if arrested, solicitors' phone numbers and so on. A system had been devised whereby every woman involved in the action would register and join a group to do non-violence training. Each gate into the base would have a legal

observer who would watch what happened, note the arrests, and relay information to a central point, via walkie-talkies hired for the purpose. All the previous afternoon women had sat huddled in caravans getting to know one another, and deciding how we'd deal with confrontation. Outside the festival had surged around, tap-dancers in radiation suits, jugglers, clowns, the Fall-Out Marching Band, all undaunted by the miserable weather. Then I had watched with amazement as 200 women in the space of an hour managed to work out how to cover seven gates for 24 hours, sleep, eat and communicate. It was going to work!

That didn't mean that I wasn't scared as my group walked out to fill the main gate at 6.30 pm: a line of police behind an enormous crowd in front and camera lights glaring in our eyes. We sat down. At six other gates women were doing the same thing, and we waited. The rain poured down steadily but the stream of traffic was absent. The base, it seemed, in consideration of our wishes, had closed itself down. So we settled in, wrapped in rugs and macs, and took turns throughout the night to do four-hour shifts. The cameramen went home. The rain turned to drizzle. Supporters brought hot tea, and entertainers, left over from the festival, went from gate to gate with fiddles and guitars.

Then in the morning, we discovered the base intended to work as usual. The police had created a new gate on a deserted bit of road. Realising that this made the rest of our blockade meaningless, some from each gate trekked round there.

'This,' the police inspector said, 'is our gate and if you sit in it you will be

arrested.' He was very courteous and gave us five minutes to think. The decision was unanimous and the first group of women sat down.

. . . The afternoon wore on. I sat in the dust at the side of the road, sun hot on my face. A line of some thirty women sat opposite me. A line of police faced them. They had changed their tactics and stopped arresting us. They were letting the traffic pile up, then swooping down and pulling us out of the way, letting us back when the traffic had passed. We had changed our tactics too. Five women were too easy to move so as many as possible had formed a strong chain. It was a wearying process. Traffic, mostly gravel trucks, came through every half hour. We were getting good at going limp but it only slowed them down. There'd been some rough treatment: pulled hair, a woman thrown to the ground, but on the whole the police had been friendly, one even sharing his fears about nuclear war with us. Two women

were keening, they had done so steadily all afternoon, wailing, 'No more war, this isn't a game, think what you're doing.'

'We were determined,' Sarah said later, 'that our vision, not theirs, should be in control of that space.'

It was growing cold, sun low and red in the sky, the police were pulling barbed wire back across the gap, they were leaving. All the women started shouting and hugging each other. 'We've done it! We've done it.' Singing and dancing we formed a circle. Then suddenly, spontaneously, silence fell. We stood filling the road. A policeman giggled, but then muffled his radio. They were silent too, for the first time that afternoon with us, not against us.

'Pass a smile around,' a woman whispered in my ear grinning. I whispered to my neighbour and watched as the women's faces lit up.

by *Lynne Jones*

Write your own important chapter. Give it a title that best sums up what it means to you.

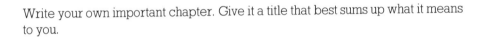

Key words

autobiographical
incidents feelings
memories experiences
challenges
development details
remember select
material personal
geographical historical
impression

Key questions (for pages 13/14)

1 What makes the dialogue in this piece different? How does the author make it more individual?
2 What is the most significant detail in the writer's otherwise vague memories of a kitchen? Does it matter that there are not more details?
3 Which details in this description of a house do you find most effective?
4 In what way is the writer's past and present linked together in this memory?
5 What makes this feel almost like poetry? What is the writer feeling at the moment of writing?

Key techniques

- using the first person in autobiographical writing (*I* [not *she*] remember . . .)
- using the past tense
- writing about strong feelings and powerful memories
- using details to bring your writing alive
- recording first experiences
- giving your memories a historical or geographical setting
- recreating real dialogue
- reflecting on your past with the knowledge of how things might have turned out differently
- recreating the background to your memories by using effective description

Manuals and guides

Writing about an interest that you have involves communicating clearly to someone the essential features of your subject and your feelings about it.

Read these two descriptions.

Slaughtering

In most parts of Britain at least, there is a public slaughterhouse somewhere in the vicinity; although these get fewer and fewer and further and further as the great philosophy of the twentieth century – Bigger Means Better – has its sway. Where at one time a bullock was quietly walked a mile or two to the village slaughterhouse, rested in the butcher's paddock for the night, and knocked on the head the next morning, now he is crammed into the back of a huge cattle-truck with thirty others, banged and lurched, terrified, over up to a hundred miles of roads, forced bellowing into a blood-reeking meat factory and eventually slaughtered. All in the sacred name of Progress.

However, if there is a slaughterhouse not too far away you can send your pig, or pigs, there and have them slaughtered for a fee. You have to get them in there though, pay for the job to be done, and go and fetch the meat back again. You make, in other words, four journeys. It is therefore very much better, if you can, to slaughter them yourself.

In most real country districts there is at least one man who will kill you a pig for a small fee. He makes it part of his living. Or perhaps there is a friendly village butcher who will do it for you. If you can entertain such a

man with friendship and home brewed beer he will do it more willingly, and be the more likely to come and do it again. Pig killing may seem to the townsman to be a brutal and grisly business, but in fact the occasion can have a kind of boozey, bucolic, charm.

I kill my pigs with a .22 rifle which I claim is the most humane method there could be. I have killed three pigs a year for sixteen years and only once (when I first began) did I have to use a second shot. I lure the pig quietly out of his sty into the cowshed with a little food in a bucket (he has had no supper the night before) and put the food into a dish. As the pig starts to eat the food I shoot him in the brain. Anywhere in the head will stun him actually, but I always shoot him in the brain. Draw a line with your imagination from his left ear-hole to his right eye, and from his other ear-hole to his other eye, and where the two lines cross, shoot him. You could not shoot him thus with a humane killer because he would not stand still for you. As soon as you put the humane killer near his head he would move away. Therefore if you use a humane killer you will have to *rope* your pig (getting a slipping noose in his mouth and round his snout) and he will squeal and struggle, and his last moments will be violent and unhappy and not perfectly peaceful as they should be. The .22 is by far the kindest way to kill a pig. One moment he is happily eating – the next moment he is in Heaven.

Immediately you have shot him stick him in the front of the neck. The place to stick seems easy to see in practice. Suffice to say that you should use a shortish knife (6 inches is long enough), stick it two inches in front of his breastbone at an angle of 45 degrees from the horizontal line of the pig and *keep it dead central*. You can easily feel the breastbone if you are in doubt, then remember, insert the knife two inches in front of it and at an angle of 45 degrees up towards the back of the pig. Thus will you cut both the carotid arteries and the jugular vein. Two things will happen. One is that blood will gush out in great quantity and now is the time for your wife to be at hand to catch it in a basin if she wants to make black pudding and has a stronger stomach than most people's wives (our blood goes down the drain I am afraid), and, secondly, the pig will begin to kick as though it is trying to win the Grand National. Let it kick, and remember it can feel nothing – its soul is in Heaven playing a porcine harp. If your wife has caught the blood, incidentally, she must stir it or whip it immediately otherwise it will clot.

We thereupon haul our pig up on a tackle, to make sure that all the blood drains out. Most people don't bother.

Cooking

Probably the most important use of fires in a survival situation (after the long list of other uses) is to cook food. Assuming that you are not surviving on Compo or MRE-type rations where most of the cooking has already been done for you, you are going to want to cook a variety of foods. The following are a variety of means by which different cooking methods can be used in a situation where you have minimal kit.

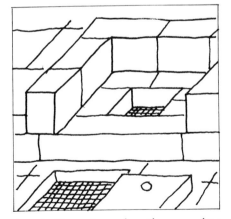

A primitive stone hearth, complete with ash pit under the fireplace and cover for the ash pit. This set-up might be used in an extended survival situation. Fruit, meat, vegetables and fish can all be baked in the ashes.

Slow fire cooking

When you wish to bake something the average camp-fire is little short of a disaster. To bake you need to have dry heat in an enclosed space. Ordinarily this is a bit difficult to arrange with a camp-fire, but it can be done. The simplest form of baking is done by placing the food inside a metal container such as a bucket, tin-box or even an oven improvised from bits of corrugated iron or sheet steel. I entitle this section slow fire cooking as it's not really the fire so much as the glowing embers and hot ashes which impart the heat.

This form of cooking is ideal when using peat fires, which are gentle fires, and it's difficult to get a good blaze with peat without resorting to a hearth combined with a shadrack, which is a rotary fan which blasts air into the peats to get them to burn fast.

As per the diagram, you can set your tin-box or container on a hearth stone and then build a peat fire over this. Alternatively, by dint of digging a hole at the side of a fire and placing your inverted bucket into it, you can have a continual supply of hot ashes raked on to the bucket, thus filling up the pit.

If you want high-temperature baking then you would set the box actually into the wood fire; in fact you would build the fire over the box. In actual fact, there were at one time iron-bake pans manufactured which would sit under a fire. The effect is of a miniature oven and it is ideal for breads and slow-cooking food, such as casseroles.

The hot ashes are an ideal place to cook baked potatoes (either in silver foil or without it), fish wrapped in either silver foil or seaweed, or even

meat. If nothing else is to hand you can wrap meat in leaves and then slap mud over the leaves and put the mud ball into the embers of the fire. I'm told (but have never tried myself) if you put hedgehog after gutting into a mud ball, that once it's cooked, which takes 1½ to 2 hours, the spines come off together with the skin when the ball is broken open. It tastes, again I'm told, like a creamy chicken. (PS Don't hunt hedgehog unless it's a real survival situation; the poor little blighters are having a tough enough time surviving cars.)

An improvised slow oven, a tin-box in a pit next to the fire. Regularly rake ashes and embers out of the fire on to the box. If you set the box on stones you can use a stick to rake ashes under the box so that it is heated from all sides.

To get a better heat the fire could be lit on logs placed above the hole with the box in it. As the logs burn through, the hot ashes and embers fall into the pit.

1 Make notes on the two passages, like this:

> ## HOW TO KILL A PIG
> 1 Starve pig
> 2 Next day lure pig into cowshed using food in bucket
> 3 etc…

2 In groups compare the methods chosen by the two writers to present their information. Think about who the writers are writing for, the language they use, and how they present the information.

3 In groups, make a list of all the information you have picked up about the attitudes of the writers of these two pieces. Do you think they feel strongly about their subjects? What makes you think this?

4 Do you have any sympathy for the views and feelings displayed by the writers? Explain why you have that reaction.

When communicating how to do something to an 'ordinary' person there are a variety of techniques you can use to make your message clearer.

Compare these two guides on giving up smoking.

Giving up smoking

How to Give Up Smoking

1 Think about stopping

The big question is: do you *really* want to stop? Because this is the key to success. Make up your mind you are going to stop, and you will. Lots of people have been surprised how *easy* it was to stop once they had really made up their minds.

To help you make your decision, think about what you gain by stopping:

Right away

- You will be free from an expensive and damaging habit.
- You'll have another £5–£10 a week to spend.
- You'll smell fresher. No more bad breath, stained fingers or teeth.
- You'll be healthier and breathe more easily – for example, when you climb stairs or run for a bus.
- And you'll be free of worry that you may be killing yourself.

For the future

- You will lose your smoker's cough.
- You will suffer fewer colds and other infections.
- And you will avoid the dangers that smokers have to face.

Many people killed by smoking could have lived 10, 20, even 30 or more years longer. On average, people killed by smoking lose 10 to 15 years of their lives.

Among 1,000 young men who smoke, about 6 will be killed on the roads but about 250 will be killed before their time by tobacco.

Women who smoke when they are pregnant run a greater risk of miscarriage or of their baby being born premature or underweight.

If you stop smoking before you have got cancer or serious heart or lung disease from smoking, then you will avoid nearly all the risks of death or disability from smoking.

Family and friends

Once you stop smoking, your family and friends gain too.
- They can enjoy fresher air.
- You'll be nicer to be with. Remember the slogan 'Kiss a non-smoker and taste the difference.'
- Children who live in smoke-free homes are much less likely to get colds and even pneumonia.
- If you don't smoke, your children are less likely to start.
- And although the main risk of smoking is to the smoker, non-smokers who live with a smoker have a higher chance of getting chest diseases.

For you, your family and friends, the benefits of stopping start on the day you stop smoking, and go on for good.

You'll be free of the worry that you may be killing yourself.

From *The Sunday Times New Book of Body Maintenance*

TIPS FOR GIVING UP

There is no magic way of giving up smoking. People find their own ways to give up. But many ex-smokers – both heavy and light smokers, young and old – have found this general advice helpful.

1 Prepare yourself

Think about when and where you usually have a cigarette. Is it in breaks at work or at home? With friends in the pub? After a meal? Once you've stopped smoking, these times and places are going to be the danger spots, so work out now how you're going to deal with them.

Plan to change your routine, or to keep yourself busy, so that you avoid the situations where you're more likely to want to smoke. For example, if you smoke after meals, get up as soon as you've finished eating, and do the washing up. If you smoke when you're out drinking with friends, skip going to the pub for a week or two.

You won't have to change your routine for ever – just for a few weeks until you find it easier to cope with the urge to smoke.

2 Pick a day

Set a target day for giving up. Make it a day when you will not be under much stress. It's not always easy to find a good time, but make it soon. It's easy to go on finding excuses for putting it off.

3 Stop

Give up. On your 'Give up day', just stop. Don't smoke any cigarettes.

4 Stay stopped

Take one day at a time. Every day without a cigarette is another success.

Every time you feel like smoking, remind yourself how much healthier you are now you've stopped. And wealthier too. Make sure you replace your cigarettes with something that's just for you – treat yourself with the money you've saved.

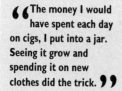

❝The money I would have spent each day on cigs, I put into a jar. Seeing it grow and spending it on new clothes did the trick.❞

20 a day for 15 years

From A Smokers Guide to Giving Up

1 In groups talk about which you find more effective and why.

2 Make a list of all the techniques used to present information about 'how to give up smoking' that were not used in the articles on survival.

3 Obtain as many manuals, guides and similar publications as you possibly can. Make a list of other techniques you find which are not illustrated here.

Beliefs

Read Paramjit Kaur's opinions on the complex situation she found herself in as a Sikh girl wishing to break free of her upbringing.

Going away to London, or rather to university was something that I had been waiting for for years.

As a first generation Sikh girl living in Britain the influences upon my life have been very different from those which have shaped the attitudes of my parents and never were the differences between us more pronounced than through my mid-teens.

My parents had always been very proud of my academic achievements. Education is always looked upon with esteem by the 'community' and therefore my getting to university only heightened this feeling of success for them. For me, university meant a chance to be free of the restrictions an Asian girl is always under and keeping my parents content at the same time.

The one thing that marred their pleasure at one of their offspring achieving a place at university was that fact that I was a girl. I come from a family of three girls and one boy, it was always expected that he would be the one to shine – to bring pride to the family. I remember vividly, the day before I left for London an aunt of mine asking my mother why it was me rather than my brother that was 'being allowed' to go to university.

Yet I had always known that if I could prove that I was capable of getting to university my parents (unlike some) would never have prevented me from doing so. That however did not mean that I went with their full enthusiasm.

Respectability is all important to an Asian family. Trying to keep the balance between staying 'respectable' and doing what I really wanted

became more and more difficult from the sixth form on, when I really began to think for myself and question everything around me more than ever.

Why was it disrespectful to argue with my father if he was wrong? Why could I not be seen with boys around the town? What was wrong with going out to clubs and drinking? Asian parents seem to have very definite ideas about what constitutes respectability and even the slightest deviation can bring the whole wrath of the community to bear. An Indian girl who is seen not to respect her parents or their ideals is looked upon by the community as being 'bad'.

There is a comment, a rather bitter one perhaps, about how an Asian girl never leaves home unless it is with a husband or in a coffin; to some degree this does sadly contain an element of truth.

My going to London was a very difficult time for my parents. Maintaining the reputation of their daughters is all important to Asian parents. The shame of a 'fallen daughter' is insurmountable. Once her reputation has in any way been marred it reflects badly upon the whole family and ultimately it will hamper her parents' attempts to arrange a marriage with a respectable Indian boy. A daughter living away from home has her respectability under question. No longer under the auspices of either her parents or the watchful community, she is susceptible to all the 'evils' that she has so far in her life been shielded from. From my own experiences I feel that this realization scares parents.

Their major fear is that their daughter will reject all they have tried to press upon her for a life which will bring shame on the family she leaves behind, and unhappiness for her. A 'badly' behaved daughter must come from a 'bad' family.

Living away from home and having the opportunity to discover various aspects of life that previously I was 'protected' from has made me realize more than ever just how subordinate to their men Indian women are. They seem to resign themselves to the fact that the men in the family will be able to dictate virtually every aspect of their lives without question. If university has taught me anything, it has been just that – to question – ruthlessly.

What perhaps I have seen to be the hardest thing of all about being an Asian girl living away from home is the choice that is to be made at the end of it all . . .

Any Asian girl in my position has had the opportunity for three or four years to discover life as it really is. Not the secure, protected, censored life of home, but a life where she can do whatever she pleases, whenever she pleases in an attempt to discover what *she* really wants and how she can get the life she wants for herself. What does she do next?

Does she reject the ideals her family hold to be 'right', does she decide that she can survive without the safety offered by the Asian society, the safety she has been used to? – or does she, as so many have done, return home and conform?

It is a hard choice to make, especially when you realize that rejecting the life your parents would want for you, a life they genuinely feel would make you happy, in effect, for most Asian girls, means rejecting your parents. A girl who refuses to conform, who openly defies her parents and the community, is a girl that any self-respecting parent would not allow to remain in their house. She has flaunted everything they stand for – she might possibly influence any other offspring to rebel

as well, and therefore must be disowned.

The affection any child feels for someone who genuinely cares and loves them and who is devoted to them is the crux of the problem. This affection and loyalty is in conflict with what you know is best for you.

For many, choosing to reject your past would mean never seeing your parents again and knowing that you are responsible for the torment and shame that they would go through.

The paradox of the whole situation and what angers me most, is that for an Asian son, his rejection of a traditional Asian life does not necessarily involve rejecting his parents. Perhaps one day this concession will include girls as well! It is a sad and confusing time for many of the Asian girls I have spoken to at university, especially for those who have realized that the one thing they can no longer accept or conform to is what symbolizes the whole Asian culture – an arranged marriage.

Many for the first time will have had the opportunity to experience a real and full relationship. One that is full of warmth and love and friendship. To be suddenly expected to convey such affection to a person that you have not been able to 'discover' and get to like is often the deciding factor for many girls regarding the choice of life they make for themselves. It will probably be so for me.

What seems to be the greatest irony of the whole situation is how parents who love and care for their daughters, parents who strive harder and harder to try and make a comfortable and happy life for their girls, can possibly look with horror or disapproval on the fact that their daughter has found happiness – by whatever means.

It is perhaps understandable that they find British life a threat to their culture, even to their religion, but the question that I often ask myself is: 'What is the point of either if it makes people unhappy?'

My parents' culture and religion

has worked well for them, but they never expected or wanted anything else. I know that I could have so much more and I am not prepared to give it up.

Any kind of education trains and encourages thought; so what is to happen as increasing numbers of Asian girls are allowed to go to university?

As this new band of independent, capable and confident young women grows, they will be able to give the help and guidance to one another that is lacking for girls like me today. That can only improve the status of Asian women, not only in the family and in the community, but in society in general, and that is something that is long overdue!

by Paramjit Kaur

▼ **Assignment 3**

1 In the opening paragraph Paramjit Kaur describes her going away to university as something she has long waited for. Describe the thing or things that you most want to do in your own life in the future.

2 In the early part of this piece much is made of the different opportunities available for girls and boys. Write about your own attitudes to this using these sub-headings to give your answer some shape.

> (a) what is described for an Asian family
> (b) what happens in your own family
> (c) what you think ought to happen in the Britain of the multicultural 1990s

These could form the basis for three paragraphs.

3 'Respectability is all-important to an Asian family.' What do you think this means? Describe what makes up your own parents' view of respectability. Is it to do with . . . girl/boyfriends? clothes? hair? their parents? wealth? agreeing with what they want? or what?

4 Describe your own feelings about the possibility of living away from home. You could draw on any experiences you have of spending time away from home.

5 A paradox is a contradiction, for example, 'being cruel to be kind'. What are the paradoxes that Paramjit Kaur describes in this passage? Do you sympathize with her? Explain why you have these feelings.

6 A 'band of independent, capable and confident young women' is described at the end of this. What qualities do you think are important for the kind of woman described here?

7 Without it becoming a story, an argument or a guide to coping with a family, Paramjit Kaur has managed to communicate her opinions clearly and individually. Now it's your turn. Write about something in your own family life that you currently feel strongly about. This could be a strong opinion that you hold, or an issue that you like to talk about, or just a pet hate of yours. Write no more than 200–300 words.

How to make Static surprises

Micky and the monster gang have discovered some snappy experiments to impress their rivals, the Roughcut Reptiles. Try them out. You will find that strange, almost magic things will happen.

Micky's pool of piranhas

Give them gaping jaws and sharp teeth so they look like piranha fish.

Cut out 20 to 30 paper fish, each about 3cm long. Put them in a plastic container with a transparent lid.*

Rub a plastic ruler with a woolly scarf quite briskly for about 10 seconds.

Slide the ruler across the lid. Watch the piranha fish jump from the bottom of their 'pool' up to the lid.

Sticky surprises

Comb your hair very fast. Hold the comb above your head and look in a mirror to see what happens.

Rub a plastic spoon with a woolly scarf and hold it near a trickle of water. The water bends towards the spoon.

The monster moves towards the ruler as if it is sitting up.

Cut out a tissue paper monster. Rub a plastic ruler on your sleeve and hold it over the monster's head.

*Micky used a mould-flavour mousse container, but you could use an empty margarine tub.

What is happening?

All these experiments happen because of static electricity. Static electricity is not the same as electricity you use at home. You can make it by rubbing things together, as shown below.

Plastic and nylon hold static electricity better than other substances.

These uncharged scraps of paper are attracted to the balloon and stick to it.

When you rub something it becomes "charged" with static electricity. When something is charged with static electricity, it pulls or attracts things that are not charged, like the scraps of paper in this picture.

Crackles and sparks

Clutty Putty is tap-dancing in plastic-soled clodhoppers. She rubs her feet on the carpet, then touches a metal radiator. Do this yourself. You may feel a tiny shock of static electricity running through your body.

Feeling static

When you undress, you can sometimes hear crackling noises. If it's dark, you may even see tiny sparks. This is static electricity made by your clothes rubbing together.

Flashes of lightning are giant sparks of static electricity.

How to make a Buzzy bee balloon

The buzzy bee balloon whizzes round and round in the air, making a loud buzzing noise. Hogwash and Micky show you how to make it.

How to make a buzzy bee balloon

Long, sausage shape balloons work best.

For the bee's body the monsters use a yellow balloon. Micky draws black stripes all over it and adds two blobs for eyes. Hogwash cuts out tissue paper wings. He makes them quite big so they are the right size when the balloon is blown up.

Use tiny bits of sticky tape to attach the wings.

Then they blow up the balloon. Hogwash holds the end tight and Micky sticks on the wings.

You can blow up the balloon and make it fly again and again.

Let go of the balloon and watch the bee buzz about. It will whizz around until all the air inside it has gone.

How the balloon flies

Scientists describe the way the balloon flies as 'action and reaction'. This means that movement in one direction causes movement in the opposite direction.

The buzzing noise is the air rushing out of the balloon.

When you let go of the balloon, the air rushes backwards out of it. This causes a reaction which pushes the balloon forwards.

Did you know?

Rockets and jets work in the same way. Hot gases rush out backwards. This pushes them forwards.

28

1 In groups, discuss and then agree on the age range you think the book these pieces come from is aimed at.

2 Make a list of all the words you would select from the pieces to support the decisions you have just taken.

3 What techniques used here seem particularly relevant to this age group? List them.

▼ Assignment 4

Make up a lively guide to an activity that you think would be of particular interest to a younger person.

Some possible ideas

How to avoid doing the washing up. . .

How to get money from your parents. . .

How to make. . .

Hints

●Divide your guide into sections with clear headings.
●If you wish, illustrate your guide.
●Make clear the age range you are aiming at.

Key words

information message manual guide attitude sub-headings illustration

Key techniques

●selecting the essential features of an activity
●putting essential features of an activity in order
●using a specialized vocabulary
●communicating your own enthusiasm/involvement in an activity
●using sub-headings
●using illustrations
●using a direct style of presentation
●using a variety of techniques

Being able to handle ideas and produce a good, convincing argument are important skills to develop. Understanding and using the different techniques of persuasion will help you to improve your own writing.

Read these two pieces. Both are written by school students and both are the opening sections of an argument about important issues.

The abuse of animals

Animals are savagely used and subjected to a considerable amount of unnecessary suffering in the name of necessity, or under the title of progress and civilization. But does progress have to involve the needless suffering of animals? Do we, in the name of technological advance, have to destroy the animal kingdom? There is no doubt that humanity is inflicting massive suffering on animals who are totally at our mercy. Animals and birds are blinded by acids, subjected to repeated shocks, poisoned, inoculated with diseases, frozen, starved and amputated internally and externally and this is all carried out in the name of 'human progress'.

Every day of the year, millions of animals are slowly blinded, tortured, frozen to be revived and re-frozen, starved or left to die of thirst, in many cases after various glands have been entirely or partially destroyed. The victim's reactions are recorded. Their suffering may last for weeks, months or years, before death puts an end to their ordeal – death being the only effective relief the victims get to know. Often, these animals are not left in peace then. No, they are brought back to life – miracle of modern science – they are then subjected to a brand new series of tortures.

Monkeys are used increasingly as the nearest substitute for humans, not only to test vaccines, nerve gases or new forms of surgery, but to discover reactions to injury in crashing motor cars. Pregnant baboons have been used to assess the effects of car seat belts on expectant human mothers who may be involved in head-on car crashes. Yet, it is plainly obvious – I should think – that baboons are not of human weight or proportion and their arms and legs are formed differently and therefore react differently under crash conditions. This, however, does not appear to be important to the scientists who are obviously under the impression that baboons are perfect human models. Monkeys are tested for just about everything from the effects of heavy smoking to exposure to atomic rays after nuclear explosions. They are also made to suffer electric shock treatment, given gastric ulcers, malaria and rabies.

from an essay by *Tanya Nyari*

Private education

'From each according to his ability, to each according to his needs.'

This is a very famous statement, said by Karl Marx, and when this is presented to anyone (including any politician), there is no way that they can directly argue against its sense and logic. Equality is a developing thing in the western world and private education is an idea which completely contradicts equal rights. If an egalitarian form of society is achieved, then everyone should have the chance to develop to the best of their ability.

Education does not mean learning only the academic subjects of life but the social ones too. How is anyone supposed to socialize with different people of different religions, different sexes, races, cultures and different social classes (at the time of your life – teenagehood – when an impression of other social circles is imposed in the strongest way) if you are separated into a school where you don't meet these different types of people? And because reality is unknown, a fantasy image is formed in the head, showing small fragments of the bad points, which have been received by mouth, and have been put together to form the completely wrong idea of the kind of person you haven't actually met before.

Is it fair that this small section of children should be given a headstart in life due to their parents' financial qualifications? I definitely don't think so, and once these children have entered into the small world of private schools, they are made to work intensively for one exam after another leading up to the big one – the entrance exam to Oxford and Cambridge. As they are trained so thoroughly for this, they have a tremendous advantage over state school children. This can be proved by statistics; approximately 58% of people accepted into either Oxford or Cambridge are privately educated, while only 7% of schools in this country are private. This is ridiculously unjust.

from an essay by *Dominique Walker*

1 In groups talk about these pairs of lines from the two arguments. For each pair agree:
   a) what they have in common
   b) what they contribute to the argument.

A 'But does progress have to involve the needless suffering of animals?'
'Is it fair that this small section of children should be given a headstart in life due to their parents' financial qualifications?'

B 'This is a very famous statement . . . and when this is presented to anyone (including any politician), there is no way that they can directly argue against its sense and logic.'
'There is no doubt that humanity is inflicting massive suffering on animals who are totally at our mercy.'

C 'No they are brought back to life, <u>miracle of modern science</u> . . .'
'and when this is presented to anyone (<u>including any politician</u>) . . .'

D 'Every day of the year, millions of animals are slowly <u>blinded</u>, <u>tortured</u>, <u>frozen</u> to be <u>revived</u> and refrozen . . .'

'Different <u>religions</u>, different <u>sexes</u>, <u>races</u>, <u>cultures</u> and different <u>social classes</u> . . .'

Comments on these lines can be found on page 43.

2 In groups, choose one of these two extracts. In what ways do you think it is an effective opening to an argument? List them.

When you argue a case one of your most effective weapons is your choice of vocabulary.

Choosing your words

I Compare these two opinions about a typical newspaper headline. In pairs make a list of all the words that seem to you to be deliberately chosen to express an attitude.

> # Exminster Council give £50,000 to aid centre.

Typical of the Loony left to go throwing our money away on a group of lazy scroungers...

It's good to know that Exminster can still show its generosity so promptly to this worthwhile cause...

Some words are clearly *positive* and helpful to a cause, while others are chosen to be critical or *negative*.

2 In pairs, put this list of words into two columns, one headed positive, one negative. Talk about any you find hard to place in one category only.

kind	simplistic	bogus	civilized
mean	posh	admirable	barbaric
thick	disgraceful	nut-case	cruel
inhuman	noisy	spendthrift	sympathetic
racist	lively	generous	sophisticated

▼ Assignment 5

Something important and newsworthy has happened in your local area. If possible this should be a real event.

Stage 1
▼
Decide what it is.
For example:
A doctor has said she will no longer accept patients who smoke.
or
Your local shop, cinema and school are going to be demolished to make way for a new by-pass.

Stage 2
▼
Assemble a list of neutral information about your chosen situation. For example:
the history behind it
a diary of events
plans, evidence, details, etc.

Stage 3
▼
Make two lists, one of positive and one of negative descriptive words and phrases to use about your chosen situation.

Stage 4
▼
Write two articles for a local newspaper, one supportive and one hostile. Express your arguments and opinions as clearly as possible. Make your vocabulary work for you. (Use the lists you have just made.) Make up strong headlines for your pieces. Use columns as they are used in a newspaper. (See Unit 4.)

Words alone do not make a good argument. It is also important to develop your ideas clearly.

Developing your ideas

1 The RSPCA was founded in 1824 to prevent the cruelty to animals that Tanya Nyari argues is taking place now in the name of 'human progress'. The RSPCA regularly produces pamphlets to put over its arguments as briefly and effectively as possible. In 1986 it was campaigning to persuade the Government to strengthen its proposals for improving animals' welfare. Its arguments are printed below, but not in the correct order. In pairs decide which order of paragraphs allows ideas to develop most clearly.

The original order can be found on Page 43.

A Therefore the RSPCA demands stricter legal controls and tougher measures to end suffering as quickly as possible.

B Now the Government is proposing changes in the law. You can help the RSPCA to get the best deal for laboratory animals by writing to your MP NOW supporting the new Government proposals in principle but asking that they be strengthened to meet RSPCA demands.

C All this − and more − is done in the name of research. About half this research is conducted for medical reasons; the rest has other purposes. And only one-fifth of all the experiments performed are carried out to satisfy the requirements of safety laws.

D Each year millions of animals suffer and die in British laboratories. Some have irritant chemicals dropped into their eyes; others have tumours implanted in their bodies.

E The Government's proposals go some way towards improving conditions for laboratory animals and experimentation procedures − but not far enough.

F Often questionable end results are made to justify painful and distressing means. Sometimes alternative tests are available.

G Sometimes animals are fed poisonous substances, or are deliberately infected with diseases. In some experiments, infant monkeys are deprived of their mothers.

This is a useful exercise which you can do using your own draft writing. Cut it up into sections and see if your partner can put it in the correct order.

2 Make a list of about six main points that *you* would make on one of these topics. Pay particular attention to your first and last points.
Either
Television is a harmful invention which the world could easily do without.
Or
Young people are not criminals by nature, but if they don't have jobs they will inevitably become so.

Well look this isn't an argument!
Yes it is!
No it isn't, it's just contradiction!
No it isn't!
It is!
It is not!
Look you just contradicted me!
I did not!
Oh you did!
No, no, no!
You did just then!
Nonsense!
Oh look, this is futile!
No it isn't!
I came here for a good argument!
No you didn't, you came here for an argument.
Well an argument isn't just contradiction.
It can be!
No it can't. An argument is a
connected series of statements
intended to establish a proposition.
No it isn't!
Yes it is! It's not just contradiction!
Look, if I argue with you I must take up a contrary position.
Yes, but that's not just saying, 'No it isn't'.
Yes it is!
No it isn't! Argument is an
intellectual process.

In conversation with someone it is easy to disagree with everything said, in this case to be deliberately difficult!

> Argument **is** an intellectual process as well as involving the emotions. One of the simplest devices to learn is to anticipate what your opponent will say and have an answer ready.

Having your answers ready

For example: *TV is a harmful invention . . .*

Background: You believe TV is a good thing, but you are worried that the weakest part of your argument is concerned with 'copycat' killings where a murderer copies something seen in a thriller or documentary . . .

You anticipate: . . . some newspapers carry stories about killers who have apparently learned how to make a bomb from watching TV. Certainly this is an area where TV must take care to be responsible, but no one could suggest that TV makes people into murderers. If you have decided to kill someone you'll do so anyway. If you didn't use a bomb you'd buy a gun or find out how to use poison . . . .

The point: If you're going to murder you'll do it anyway, not because of TV.

1 In pairs:
   a) Think of three other strong arguments on this subject, to support the view that TV is not harmful.

b) For each one then think of the counter arguments (that TV *is* harmful) you would produce.

c) Then think of a way of answering each counter argument so that your case (that TV *isn't* harmful!) is strengthened.

2 For each of these statements anticipate a strong counter argument. Then produce an answer to the counter argument and write up a brief statement of your own including this answer. Read them out to others in the group.

    a) Fashion is a gimmick invented by shops to sell more clothes.

    b) To smoke or not is a matter for individuals to decide.

    c) Living near a nuclear power station is safer than crossing a typical high street.

> **Starting an argument well is as important as writing a good first line in a story or getting the attention of your listeners if you are speaking.**

How to start

1 In groups rank these opening sentences in order of how effective you think they are. Each one is arguing for equal opportunity for women. Agree what kinds of openings you think are most effective.

A 'Frailty thy name is woman': what a ridiculously unscientific statement this is, yet we still hear men trotting it out as if they are lord of the manor.

B There are many women who are very capable of doing jobs which traditionally are performed by men.

C As I was sitting on the top floor of a number 19 bus the other day an elderly woman turned to me and whispered that she thought she got on much better these days now her old man had left her.

D Half the world is female and yet there are only a handful of women directors, surgeons and Members of Parliament.

E Women may have the vote these days but they don't have much else.

F In this essay I am going to argue that there should be equal opportunities for men and women.

G I think that women are better than men.

2 Choose the opening sentence you found most effective and say why.

3 Write the first three paragraphs for an essay on this subject, assuming that you are preparing for a debate or class discussion.

Try to use these skills:

- choosing questions well
- expressing opinions as if they were facts
- choosing vocabulary carefully
- developing ideas logically
- anticipating arguments

Assignment 6

You are going to produce a piece of coursework on the topic of equal opportunity. The assignment will be based on a speech you have given in class.

Stage 1 Find out some information to support aspects of the topic that interest you.

Stage 2 Decide what your opinions are on the subject of equal opportunity. You might want to ask others in the group or mothers or grandmothers or your friends.

Stage 3 Using your paragraphs from 3 as draft material, adapt and extend them to write out in full a speech on this subject.

Stage 4 Have a class discussion on this subject.

Stage 5 For your final piece of coursework, redraft your speech in the light of anything you have learned by talking through the issues.

Statistics

Burning Up Calories

By eating a 4 oz (approx. 100g) bar of milk chocolate about 660 calories are added to your daily total. If these are in excess of daily requirements, the length of time it takes to burn them off may make you think twice before indulging. If you don't burn off the calories they become body fat — 3 oz per chocolate bar. Exercise will burn off calories — but it takes longer than you think. To indulge in an extra bar of chocolate without gaining extra weight, one of the following activities should be performed for the time shown.

Activity	Duration
Walking at 4mph	2 hours 10 minutes
Cycling at 13mph	1 hour
Driving a car	4 hours
Digging the garden	1 hour 20 minutes
Swimming 20 yards a minute	50 minutes
Ironing clothes	2 hours 40 minutes

1 Which of these statements about these simple statistics are true? Which are false? Which are *possible* interpretations of the statistics?

a) Every 4oz chocolate bar you eat will produce 3oz of body fat.
b) If you eat a 4oz chocolate bar you will be able to iron for 2 hours 40 mins.
c) Driving a car for 4 hours is the same as swimming 20 yards a minute for 50 minutes.
d) Digging the garden for 1 hour 20 minutes will burn off 3oz body fat.
e) If you drive a car for eight hours a day you should eat two 3oz chocolate bars.

THERE ARE LIES, DAMNED LIES AND STATISTICS

Disraeli

Your ability to use statistics and other information to favour your case will be a great advantage. You will also be better at detecting tricks played on you by selective use of facts!

2 Study these statistics about the votes received by some imaginary political parties. The Mauve Party has just won a General Election!

	1987	Election now
Mauve Party	35%	40%
Drive on the right Party	10%	0%
Free beer Party	15%	5%
Stop smoking on the buses Party	1%	2%
Silly Party	5%	7%
Rude Party	20%	28%
(NB Non-voters)	14%	18%

If you wanted to argue that the *Stop smoking on the buses Party* had done very well you could say:

We had a very successful election and managed to double our vote. (Still only 2%!)

If you were a member of the Mauve Party you might put it like this:

Only a pathetic 2% of the electorate voted for stopping smoking on the buses, which means that 98% of people want smoking to continue.

(This might not be true!)

Use these statistics to argue that:
  a) The Silly Party has done well.
  b) The Silly Party has done badly.
  c) The country is getting ruder.
  d) The Mauve Party is not in the majority.
  e) People still want free beer.

See what else you can get the statistics to say!

Assignment 7

Stage 1 Choose a topic from this list.
Racism
Nuclear weapons
Poverty
Happiness
Road safety

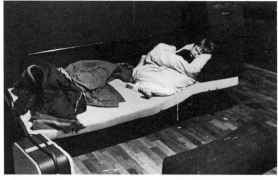

Stage 2 Make a list of some possible titles for one of these topics. Decide for whom you are writing, for example, people your own age, family, local Primary school, pamphlet, etc. Decide what your purpose is. Choose the most suitable title from your list.

Stage 3 Brainstorm your ideas on your chosen subject. Start listing words which you think will be particularly useful in your argument. (You may need to refer back to page 32.)

Stage 4 Find out and make notes of any 'evidence' you intend to use. This could take the form of statistics, pictures, newspaper cuttings, etc. Decide how you are going to use this evidence.

Stage 5 Find at least one suitable quotation to support your argument.

Stage 6 Shape your information into a first draft. This will involve:
● deciding on an order for your information,
● producing a strong opening paragraph,
● deciding how to end your argument.

Stage 7 Read your argument aloud to a particular partner and then make any necessary changes as a result of this.

Stage 8 Check that you have used as many of the techniques illustrated in this Unit as possible.

Stage 9 Produce your final draft and, if possible, try it out on the audience you had in mind in Stage 2!

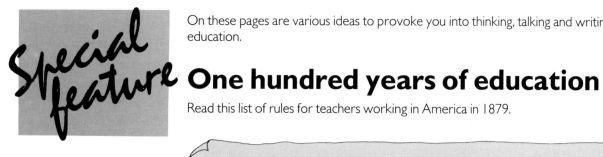

On these pages are various ideas to provoke you into thinking, talking and writing about education.

One hundred years of education

Read this list of rules for teachers working in America in 1879.

1) *Teachers each day will fill lamps, clean chimneys, before beginning work.*

2) *Each teacher will bring a bucket of water and scuttle of coal for the day's session.*

3) *Make your pens carefully; you may whittle nibs to the individual taste of the children.*

4) *Men teachers may take one evening a week for courting purposes or two evenings to attend church regularly.*

5) *After 10 hours in school you may spend the remaining time reading the Bible or other good books.*

6) *Women teachers who marry or engage in unseemly conduct will be dismissed.*

7) *Every teacher should lay aside from each pay a good sum for his benefit during his declining years so that he will not become a burden on society.*

8) *Any teacher who smokes, uses liquor in any form, frequents pool and public halls, or gets shaved in a barber's shop, will give good reason to suspect his worth, intention, integrity and honesty.*

1 Talk about all the ways in which the life-style of a teacher must have been different then from now. Discuss any hints you receive from the rules about life for schoolchildren in 1879.

2 In groups, agree a list of the eight rules you would like to see adopted for teachers now. For each one, make sure that you could support it with sensible arguments. *Example*: Read what a fifteen-year-old student put as his first four rules.

1 No drinking of tea or coffee or any stronger form of thirst quencher during lessons, or in sight of students. This can cause distress to the student who is not allowed to drink in class.

2 Any member of staff caught wasting time — by walking slowly to lessons, leaving lessons to have a chat with other staff, pretending to lose work, losing the classroom key or not turning up at all — will be dismissed.

3 Swearing or bad use of the English language will result in a day without pay.

4 English teachers who set work during the Summer holidays will be made to copy out the complete works of Shakespeare... in German.

3 Compare your ideas with some of the Secretary of State for Education's in 1987.

The Government proposes to incorporate provisions that:

- a teacher may be required to work on not more than **195** days a year, of which **190 days** shall be days on which he or she may be required to teach pupils;

- a teacher may be required to work for **up to 1,265** hours a year at specified times and places at the direction of the head teacher;

- a teacher may not be required to undertake **midday supervision**, and shall be entitled to a break of reasonable length during the school day;

- unless employed as a supply teacher, or timetabled to undertake specific duties for less than 75% of the school week, or if no supply teacher is available, a teacher would not normally be required to **cover for an absent colleague** after the absent teacher has been away from school for 3 days; nor to cover for a planned absence of more than 3 days.

- a teacher will work **such additional hours** as may be necessary to discharge his or her professional duties: teachers will decide when and where to undertake such work.

4 In groups prepare a similar list for students in schools now.

5 Make up some questions to ask older members of your family about what school was like 'in their days'. (Note down the answers when you do this.)

Sexism in schools

Schools for the Boys? is the title of a book which argues that schools are biased against girls. Do you agree with this idea? Think about this before reading on.

1 In groups talk about this extract from a widely-used maths textbook.

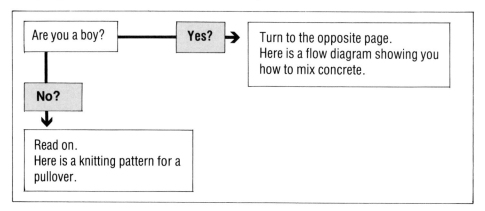

2 Why do you think few boys study subjects like home economics, and few girls study physics?

3 Talk about any conclusions you draw from this set of statistics.

	Boys %	Girls %		Total entries
		100	Needlework	24,459
	8	92	Business & Office Practice	24,278
	31	69	Biology	208,548
	36	64	Music	11,206
	37	63	French	163,326
	40	60	Religious Knowledge	55,573
	48	52	Mathematics	419,238
	50	50	English	666,125
Art & Craft	52	48		173,468
Geography	59	41		194,630
Chemistry	61	39		129,520
Computer Studies	63	37		58,279
Physics	78	22		148,661
Technical Drawing	94	6		78,619
Woodwork	97	3		38,596

The percentage distribution of boys and girls in examinations at 16+ (1985)   Source DES

4 Answer these questions:
  a) How many books have you read this year by women?
  b) How many books have you read this year in which women have important jobs?
  c) How many of your school's senior staff are women?
  d) How important are girls in your school? (if it is mixed sex)

 **Assignment 8**

Stage 1 In groups make up a questionnaire to find out from your class:
  a) how many of their mothers work
  b) what jobs they do
  c) what jobs the girls in your class would like to do
  d) what jobs the boys in your class would like to do
  e) other relevant information about how girls are treated in your school
  You will need to make up several questions to obtain this information.

Stage 2 Organize your results into a chart or a set of statistics.

Stage 3 Write some accompanying paragraphs in which you state your viewpoint. Write it in language that will be understood by other students in your school.

Stage 4 Add a final paragraph headed *Some Recommendations*.

Stage 5 Make a final draft of this in the form of a pamphlet. Make it as attractive as possible.

Discussion

In groups choose two of these statements.
Discuss them fully as preparation for a piece of individual writing.

All schools should have an elected student council.
School uniform is a relic of the past.
No school needs a headteacher these days.
You don't need rules in a modern school.
Teachers today are too soft.
Boys shouldn't have to learn cookery and textiles.
There should be more female physics teachers.
Teachers should be called by their first names.
Students should use the same toilets as teachers.
All schools should teach the same subjects.
After the age of 14 there should be a completely free choice of subjects for all students.
Examinations should be abolished.
Students should be paid for staying on after the age of 16.
Religious assemblies should be abolished.
All students should have to learn about major world religions and life-styles, regardless of their own.
Schools should be voluntary after lunchtime.
All students should be given free school meals.

Assignment 9   Choose one or more of the statements listed above. Make up an essay title for yourself. Develop an argument in which you explore many points of view and end by stating your conclusions. Write your essay with a view to it being read by other students *and* staff at your school.

Detailed comments on page 31

A These are known as rhetorical questions. The writer doesn't attempt to answer them. S/he assumes that the argument is developed because they do *not* have any obvious answers or because any answers given would support the cause being put forward.

B Having the confidence to present opinions as if they were facts well-known to others helps to build up confidence in your argument.

C Humour, even if bitter or mocking, helps to develop your case intelligently and present you as a person aware of 'the ways of the world'.

D A list of words of similar or related meaning adds force to your argument. This is especially effective, often in groups of three, when giving a speech.

Page 33
Original order was **DGCFBEA**

Key words

fact opinion evidence emotive prejudiced biased information conclusion therefore generalization interpretation reasoned reasonable unreasonable objective subjective case rhetorical list statistic

Key techniques

- using **rhetorical questions** (questions that are left to the reader or listener to answer)
- using **vocabulary carefully** (for example, words with an emotional appeal)
- using **deliberate tone** (for example, mocking or saying the opposite of what you mean)
- using **quotations or anecdotes**
- using **information selectively** (for example, choosing statistics which support your cause)
- developing **ideas clearly and logically**
- exploring the **implications of ideas fully**
- looking at **other points-of-view** (for example, anticipating arguments)
- starting **effectively**
- repeating **messages**
- presenting **opinions as if they were facts**

UNIT 4 *Newspapers and magazines*

Newspapers and magazines are two sources of a range of interesting non-fiction articles. This unit looks closely at reports and features.

Reports

Vengeance of a bus company clerk

By Martin Wainwright

An undercover attempt to bring romance into the bus timetables of South Wales ended yesterday in a two-month gaol sentence. Travellers who wondered why buses in the region showed an unusual turn of speed earlier this year learned the answer at Blackwood magistrates' court in Gwent.

Before the bench was Mr Tim Worel, aged 27, referred to during the hearing as 'a public pest'. The magistrates heard that Mr Worel's courting of his girlfriend Tracey had been threatened by bus connection times.

The sadness of the situation was worsened by the fact that Mr Worel, of Cefn Fforest, Gwent, was a timetable clerk for the Welsh Bus Company himself, forced to work with the very figures which mucked up his efforts to meet Tracey. His answer was simple but successful; he encouraged bus drivers he knew to speed up.

'Because he was on good terms with many of the drivers, they would be persuaded to go faster to be ahead of schedule,' said Mr Mark Powell, defending. The strategy worked well until a bad fairy — or rather an understandably irritated inspector — discovered what was going on.

Conscious that the Welsh Bus Company might get a bad name if its evening services flew past stops while people were only halfway to them. Mr Richie Young, aged 46, cracked down. Mr Worel was given a warning and the practice was stopped. But thwarted lovers can do more than pine.

'Something of a feud developed between Mr Worel and the inspector,' said Mr Powell. 'Mr Worel thought it was necessary for him to extract revenge.'

As a result, seven tons of manure, three tons of anthracite, a lorry-load of ready-mixed cement, a gas leak emergency team, an undertaker, a scrap merchant, and people replying to an advertisement offering Mr Young's car for sale arrived at the inspector's home in Cwmcarn, Gwent.

Mr Worel, who was described by Mr Powell as a man with a bizarre nature but who was also extremely intelligent, admitted five charges of carrying out hoaxes by deception and a sixth of making an annoying telephone call. He was given six concurrent sentences of two months by the magistrates' chairman, Mr John Jones, who described him as 'extremely foolish.'

From The Guardian

1 Complete this chart.

Name	Age	Occupation	Part played in the story
Mr Tim Worel			
Tracey 'X'	?		
		Bus inspector	
	?	Solicitor	

2 In pairs, have the conversation that you think Tim Worel might have had with one of his bus driver friends, trying to persuade them to go faster.

3 You are Richie Young and have just received this letter. Write a reply to it in which you apologise without giving too much away.

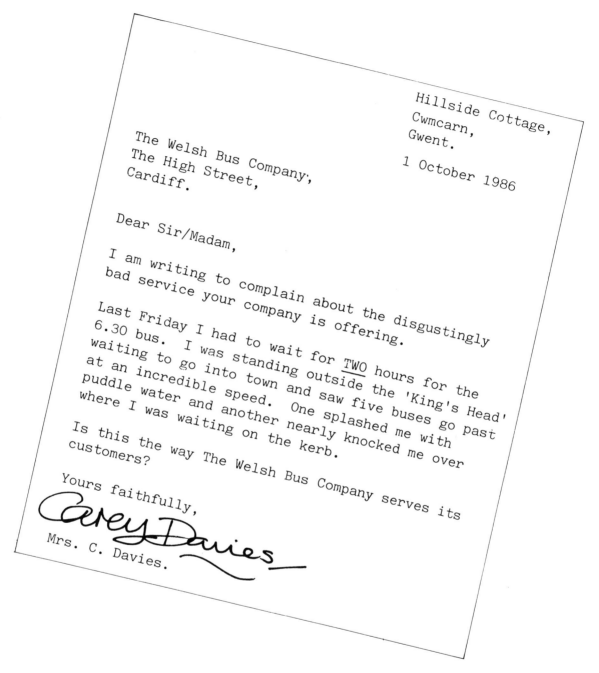

Hillside Cottage,
Cwmcarn,
Gwent.

1 October 1986

The Welsh Bus Company,
The High Street,
Cardiff.

Dear Sir/Madam,

I am writing to complain about the disgustingly bad service your company is offering.

Last Friday I had to wait for TWO hours for the 6.30 bus. I was standing outside the 'King's Head' waiting to go into town and saw five buses go past at an incredible speed. One splashed me with puddle water and another nearly knocked me over where I was waiting on the kerb.

Is this the way The Welsh Bus Company serves its customers?

Yours faithfully,

Carey Davies

Mrs. C. Davies.

4 One of Tim Worel's hoaxes involved trying to sell Mr Young's car. Compose the advertisement that might have appeared in the local newspaper.

▽ Assignment 10

Stage 1 Several other hoaxes are also mentioned. In groups develop a short scene based on ▽ *one* of them. Invent other characters to make your scene fuller and more entertaining.

Stage 2 Using your group's ideas produce a report of between 400–500 words similar to the ▽ one you have read.

Discussion

In groups, talk about these statements overheard in the Magistrates' Court.

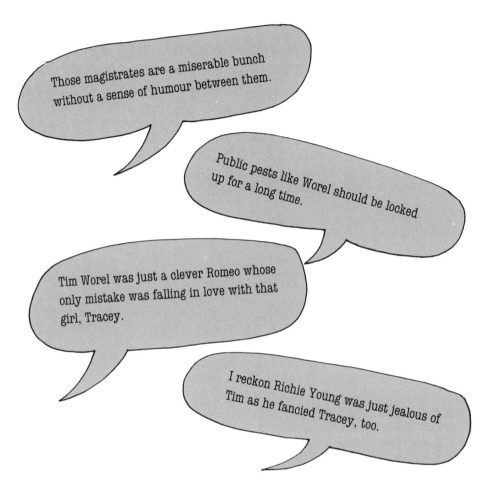

Those magistrates are a miserable bunch without a sense of humour between them.

Public pests like Worel should be locked up for a long time.

Tim Worel was just a clever Romeo whose only mistake was falling in love with that girl, Tracey.

I reckon Richie Young was just jealous of Tim as he fancied Tracey, too.

The past tense

An undercover attempt to bring romance into the bus timetables of South Wales *ended yesterday* in a two-month gaol sentence.

> **Most reports in newspapers are written in the past tense about things that happened yesterday or earlier.**

Compare these two statements about Mr Worel, the timetable clerk.

a) He was given six concurrent sentences of two months by the Magistrates' chairman, Mr John Jones, who described him as extremely foolish.

b) I was in court when he was given six concurrent sentences of two months by the Magistrates' chairman, Mr Jones. I heard Mr Jones describe him as extremely foolish.

What differences are there between the two?

> **Reports in newspapers are normally written in the past tense *and* in the third person. This makes the report seem more definite and concentrates on its subject rather than on the reporter.**

Hard times for the Cardboard City vagrants

THE MUSIC and glitter continue overhead, but conditions are getting tougher for the inhabitants of Cardboard City, the shanty town of vagrants under London's South Bank.

The colony has dwindled to between 30 and 40 hardened dossers and the only 24-hour toilet nearby is now closed at night, forcing them to use buckets.

In the shadow of the concrete arches of the Festival Hall just yards from the concert-goers there are five containers full of urine, the air is full of flies and the stench is overpowering.

This is life on the pavements in 1987. One hundred years ago Henry Mayhew, the social investigator of Victorian London, described what it was like to be down and out in the capital in *London Labour and the London Poor*.

On the centenary of his death, it seems little has changed for the inhabitants of Cardboard City.

Mayhew wrote of the vagrants queuing for admission to the Asylum for the Houseless Poor: 'It is a terrible thing, indeed, to look down upon that squalid crowd. There they stand shivering in the snow, with their thin, cobwebby garments hanging in tatters about them. Many are without shirts: with their bare skin showing through the rents and gaps of their clothes, like the hide of a dog with the mange.'

On the South Bank, life can be just as harsh. Joan and Jason Buck have lived in Cardboard City on and off for four years. Their

home — a damp and draughty patch of concrete six feet square with cardboard walls — is known as a 'basher' because it is bashed together from bits and pieces scavenged from the streets.

One side is made from an old classroom map of the world. The roof is the sloping recesses underneath the Queen Elizabeth Hall.

Despite the squalor, the Bucks are fond of the place. 'Once I lock the gate and get my head down, nobody comes near us,' says Joan, as if she were sleeping behind a suburban front door instead of the remains of a wooden packing case barely three feet high.

Their lives revolve round handouts from soup kitchens and even from Thames river boats. 'They come down here with bits of chicken and stuffed pork on little sticks, what the people on the boats don't want,' Joan says.

The vagrant colony has a close relationship with the Festival Hall authorities who help the regulars, but move on troublemakers.

The management denies suggestions that it has cracked down on the dossers. Their number always dwindles in the summer, it says.

Richard Pulford, the general director of the Festival Hall, said: 'We have no intention or wish to make their wretched lives more wretched. Every now and then we get people who turn up and don't fit in and make a terrible mess of the place, and we ask them to move on. The other dossers don't want them to stay either.'

The management says the toilets have been closed because so few people are living in Cardboard

City. Mr Pulford says they will be reopened 24 hours a day when the dossers' numbers rise in the winter.

Joan and Jason Buck have their own private bucket which they keep clean. They try their best to keep their basher tidy, draping their clothes on hangers against the back wall. Like most of the colony, they live on social security — £29.40 a week — and anything they can pick up from casual work or begging. Both are Irish, Jason, 27, from Dublin, and Joan, 47, from Limerick. They came to Britain years ago to find work, but it all went wrong.

'I'm an alcoholic, he's an alcoholic,' Joan says. 'Mind you, you have to drink down here. You get enough drink in you, you go to sleep. If you stay sober down here, you'll be a lunatic.'

They have had stints in hostels and hated them. They have tried living on a different patch.

'We used to sleep over at Hungerford Bridge, but it was really violent,' says Joan. 'You get a lot of people mugging you, you have to sleep with one eye open. They battered someone to death there for 25p.' They quickly returned to Cardboard City.

For the future, they cling to the hope that they will be given a council flat. For the present, it is a bleak and unforgiving existence.

'God knows what we will do for the rest of the day,' says Joan. 'Sit here, have a drink, do some begging.'

From *The Independent*

1 In groups, compare this more serious article with the one about the bus clerk. In particular, agree what the different effects of using the present tense are.

2 What do these details add?
   a) the paragraphs about Henry Mayhew
   b) the quotations from the Bucks
   c) the quotation from Mr Pulford
   d) the use of words like *dosser* and *basher*
   e) the ending with Joan Buck's comments

3 How sympathetic do you think the writer of this report is?

▽ Assignment 11

Find out about individuals or groups who are living in an unconventional way near you. Write an article for a local or national newspaper or magazine about them. Give your piece some kind of background against which the reader can picture your report. Make the purpose of your article clear.

Forget Smiler…

… meet David instead, and you'll never think small again

ONE of teenager David Pain's biggest ambitions is to live in America. 'I like the fast life,' he tells you — and you can't help believe him.

At 16, he's self-confident and self-motivated, with his sights firmly set on the good things in life. He seems older than his years, enjoys company and has a list of interests to put most to shame.

David is also an actor. While most of his classmates are labouring over their mock O-levels, he's swopped his school uniform for a theatre costume and a taste of the bright lights of pantomime life.

Being 4ft 5in tall, he plays Smiler in Snow White and the Seven Dwarfs at Oxford Apollo. It's his first pantomime, his most important role so far — and he's loving every minute of it.

But when his greasepaint has been taken off and the twice daily shows are over, it's back to the textbooks for him, too, at the Rose Hill guest house where he is staying during the show.

David had to get a special licence to take time off school for the pantomime, and will be sitting his exams when he returns to class early next month.

It wasn't that long ago that he first realised he could make money out of his stature — although he says it isn't just the cash benefits that attract him to the entertainment business.

His first experience of stage life was with village theatre groups, which he started when he was 11.

Then a chance encounter in his home town set him on the path to professional acting. He was walking along the road when he was approached by a woman who told him her mother was an agent. David handed over his name and address, but heard nothing more. And so he contacted Equity, which in turn suggested he call Johnny Laycock, an agent specializing in finding entertainment work for smaller people.

When he was 14, David did a few days filming for Labyrinth, but he believes the pantomime is his most important job so far.

He was born at Llanwit-major in South Wales and lived there for six years before his family moved to Cyprus.

They returned to England in the middle of 1978, and after a short spell in London, moved to Maidenhead.

David's father is a civil servant — 'something in the management side' — and his mother is a secretary working for the industrial tribunals in London. He has a 19-year-old brother Christopher, who is studying mathematics at Reading University, and a sister Julie, 18, who is at art college.

As for David, he is in the fifth year of a large Maidenhead comprehensive school. In the summer he is set to take eight O-levels and if he passes four or more, he has been offered a place at a nearby college to study art, physics and mathematics at A-level.

He has been a vegetarian for two years. He enjoys '60's mania music', hates Soul, and says he watches too much television. He enjoys skiing on snow and water, canoeing, swimming and tennis, has played rugby at school, and holds an orange belt for judo which he learned at a local community centre.

David has a very positive attitude to life, but says that when he was younger he hated the word 'dwarf'. It made him 'shudder through to the bones'.

But talking to the dwarfs during the filming of Labyrinth helped a great deal, boosting his confidence, and reaffirming that they 'were normal people — just like you.'

He says he has never had a hard time at any of the schools he had been to. He has always been welcomed and treated like anyone else, and a big party of school friends may be coming to see his Oxford performance.

His parents support him in whatever he chooses to do, although David admits that his mother is worried about the effect of stage work on his exams.

The money he earns goes towards clothes and his social life, and he manages to save quite a bit, too.

David is hoping to do more entertainment work, although he is keeping his options open about his future career. If he can't make it in front of the camera, then there is a chance that he will move behind it to the technical side of film work.

From The Oxford Times

1 Talk about the ways in which David demonstrates a 'positive attitude' to life according to this article.

2 Discuss the impression you gain of David's family.

3 What are the significant events in David's past which the writer has chosen to select?

4 Which tenses are used in this feature? What effects do they have?

5 David is in the last year of his compulsory schooling. Imagine you are the teacher responsible for careers at his Maidenhead Comprehensive School. Make up a list of the questions you would want to ask David if you were interviewing him about his future possible career after school.

6 In pairs, using your prepared questions, role play the interview that David might have with the Head of Careers in his school.

7 Write this interview out as a script.

Features about people can be written in a variety of different styles and for local or national audiences.

Assignment 12

Write a feature on somebody of your own age whom you admire. She or he could be a famous young person in the TV, Film or Theatre world, *or* somebody who is as yet unknown and *not* involved in this kind of activity.
If possible this should be based on information gained in an interview with your subject.

In the feature make it clear:

- what you like/admire about her/him

- her/his family background (choose significant details)

- her/his current interests and future plans

Include a direct quotation from your subject.

Another way of presenting a feature about a person is to include information gained by interviewing someone else as well.

In this feature, the poet and novelist Christopher Nolan and his sister Yvonne talk to Sue Fox.

Interviews

Christopher – Christy – Nolan, 21, very nearly died at birth from asphyxiation. He survived with very severe brain damage, which left him unable to speak or move. At the age of 15 Christy wrote a remarkable book of poems, *Dam-Burst of Dreams*, which was published with great success. *Under the Eye of the Clock* is Christy's story of how he succeeded in breaking through the world of silence and how he won his battle to go to university. Christy types with a unicorn stick attached to his head . . .

A will to survive

Christopher Nolan: Yvonne is my greatest ally. An early memory of my sister was the time she saved me from slipping into a bath of hot water. Mam had run the bath and left Yvonne holding me in a sitting position on the edge of the bath. An involuntary movement of my body was about to force me down into the bath, but Yvonne stepped fully clothed into the hot water, in order to place herself between me and the water. That was always her style, her forethought. It came naturally to her and to this day it still does.

Yvonne treats me as normal and because of her I am normal. Normal in my outlook on life, normal in my dealing with my friends, but above all, normal in my response in my dreadful destiny. Because she bullied me, I, too, can bully until I get my way. Assisting me always, she never put a price tag on her efforts and I always felt free to ask and ask again. By feeling free I was never shy of demanding to play in all games despite being more of a hindrance than a help.

Youth was rarely without fun. We lived all of our early years on a farm in the Irish midlands. We – Yvonne and I – spent our days playing with the children on the farm next to ours. There were 11 children in that family so they became our family too. We loved them, fought with them, we ganged up against them but, above all, we played happy games of screeching freedom with them. Trying to fit in, I experienced many a hard knock. Yvonne, though, was always at hand.

Being game to help and defend me to the death did not mean my sister was a pacifist. She was more than capable of looking after herself. Looking on always, she would only allow my parents to give me the very minimum of necessary attention. Her question, 'What about me?' was noisily shouted at busy times. To this very day, that

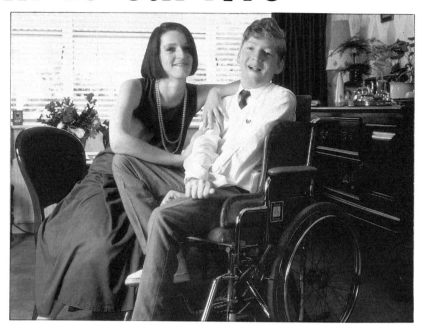

question of hers stops me from being selfish, from demanding too much attention for myself.

Without speech, I was never without a spokeswoman. Yvonne stood in for me and, reading my eye-signalled talk, she expressed my wishes for me. Parents can be square, can be nervous for their children's sake, but all I had to do was hint to Yvonne and she would say: 'Christy says he'd like to go, too,' or 'Christy says that's not the right gear for his age.' That was our method of joining together to get what we wanted. I hinted to Yvonne, or using the same eye-signals she hinted to me, and then we joined forces against our parents. We applied ourselves to choosing our own clothes, our own friends, our own music, even our own pets.

There were times when we didn't see eye to eye. A great row took place when Yvonne made her first holy communion. She forced me to stay at home, insisting that it was *her* day and 'You're not going to spoil anything for me.' I was heartbroken and begged my mother to let me go. She was on Yvonne's side and refused point blank. I remember screaming and sobbing. I

was so mad at my mother that I screamed, 'You bloody bitch!'

Disabled as I am, my fight for dignity is ever ongoing. My parents are supportive, but it is to Yvonne that I turn for advice. 'Do you think I can fit into a normal secondary school?' 'Ought I to chance my "head" at writing a book?' 'Can I master a university curriculum?' Her faith in me must come from knowing I like the challenges of life. Her replies seemed to be: 'Go on, you can do it.'

Nothing gets me down, despite my terrible handicap, but I envy my sister heading off on her magical travels. Her being able-bodied makes for freedom; my being disabled makes for wishing. I wish I could see China, Egypt, America, the Holy Land, the Australian outback or mangrove swamps. That's just wishing for the moon. My reality must necessarily be hemmed in. In my prison I can fly my thoughts to rest awhile on Mount Everest, or slip inside the Berlin Wall. Yvonne, in her travels, will know I'm there beside her, silently egging her on to glance this way or that. So we always did; why change now?

Now I'm being hailed as a writer with promise. Yvonne was the first to spot the promise in my recent book. I sent her the typescript to seek an honest opinion. 'Yes, I read it – it was brill. . . wonderful.'

My life is great now, my future is bright now, my next book is ready in my brain now, but somewhere, in the future, I know that Yvonne will perhaps marry, want to lead her own life. That I expect, that I understand and for those very reasons I want to say: 'Yvonne, all my fears are as nothing compared to my wish to set you free to live your own fashioned life.'

Yvonne Nolan: I was two years old when Christy was born and I began to feel jealous because he took up so much of my parents' time and attention. My happiest childhood memories are of the years we spent on the farm outside Mullingar. It was an idyllic childhood in some ways but there was always a great deal of sibling rivalry between me and Christy.

I was instinctively protective of him and conscious of including him whenever there were other children to play with but sometimes I thought it would have been wonderful to head off by myself down the fields.

Christy was eight when we packed up and moved to Dublin so that he could go to the Central Remedial Clinic in Clontarf. It wasn't an easy time for any of us and I was very unhappy at school. I was made to feel a real 'culchie', which is the Irish equivalent of a country bumpkin.

When anyone was invited to our house, they got a real drilling from me to prepare them for Christy. I told them that they weren't to pretend he wasn't there, that he wasn't mentally handicapped and could understand everything they said perfectly well. If somebody didn't make the effort to talk to Christy, I wasn't interested in their friendship.

When I was 12 my parents sent me away to boarding school in Banagher. After the first few weeks of congealed stews I came home for the weekend and accused my parents of wanting to get rid of me so they could devote themselves to Christy. When we sat down to talk I could see that my parents had made tremendous sacrifices to send me. It would have been much easier for them to keep me at home so I could mind Christy and give them a break. What they had done was to give me an opportunity to 'blossom' as Mum called it. One thing which made me mad was that people always brought presents for Christy and made such a fuss of him. You'd think I didn't exist. Often I never got so much as a 20p bar of chocolate.

Despite the sibling rivalry, I've always been very protective of my brother and would instinctively come to his rescue. I was so nervous for him before he started Mount Temple Comprehensive School. I knew how it would be, that 90 per cent of the kids would think he was a vegetable and make fun of him. Even if one or two were sensitive enough to recognize my brother for what he was, it would take somebody exceptional not to go with the crowd. I was afraid he would be isolated. How I underestimated Christy's resilience. Not long after Christy started at Mount Temple I could breathe easier, safe in the knowledge that now Christy had real friends to defend him.

I've always known Christy had a unique talent. Any publisher in his right mind would have recognized that here was something quite extraordinary. It is still painful for me when people lump Christy's writing with his disability. He is a writer who happens to be handicapped, not a handicapped writer. Christy says one day I'll write a book too, but I doubt if I have the talent or the discipline.

There has always been a tremendous empathy between me and my brother. When he was at Trinity and I was at University College I'd go to lectures with just a jotter and pen so that I could take out eight books from the library – four books for me and another four for Christy. From the title of his essay I'd know where to find the relevant bit to read to him.

There's nothing I couldn't do or haven't done for Christy, but I've never mollycoddled him. There were times when he had to be in hospital when I couldn't bear to see how the doctors and nurses looked after him. Christy's needs are so special and hospital usually made him worse. Mum would bring him home and between us we'd know exactly what to do for him.

All my life, I've never been simply Christy Nolan's sister. I'm Yvonne Nolan and I've never let my brother forget that. I remember my first communion when I was seven and didn't want Christy there to interfere with my day. No, I don't feel guilty. Looking back, I think we both respect each other's need for space. I don't ever want to leave Dublin for good, but I love to travel and Christy's disability has never made me feel trapped. He'd be the last one to stand in the way of me leading my own life ●

1 In groups, talk about:
 a) the ways in which Christy's life could be described as normal,
 b) the particular strengths of his relationship with Yvonne,
 c) the challenges they have faced and will continue to face. (Consider this from Yvonne's point of view too.)

2 What do you think the inclusion of Yvonne's point of view adds to our understanding of Christopher Nolan?

Sometimes a fuller impression of a person's life can be created by writing in a more general way about the kinds of activities that make up typical days.

A Life in the Day of

These two features are taken from a Sunday magazine. In them interesting people are asked to describe a typical day.

At roughly 7.30am my radio alarm buzzes. As it is actually on my bed it literally blasts me into awareness of the morning. This is due to the loudness I need to wake me. I lie for a while deciding whether to brave the bitter cold of the surrounding room or stay in bed and pretend to be fatally ill. This trick doesn't usually work, but I try anyway. My mother never believes me. This could be due to either of two factors. Either I am a very poor actress or my mother dismisses my mysterious illness as a regular occurrence.

On a school morning I usually manage to squeeze 10 minutes between my mother's and father's bathroom times. My father's reaction to anyone else being in the bathroom in 'his' bathroom time leaves much to be desired. It would be safer waving a red flag at a raging bull. I actually fear his reaction. Not that he would strike me or anything, but I think he feels both angry and hurt that he can't have the bathroom in his own home, and I wouldn't want to hurt him.

I admit I spend more than my fair share of time in the bathroom, but teenage girls need pampering time more than men. My father contradicts himself by portraying himself as an old man – too old for this and that – and then spends much time and money applying 'wet-look' styling gel to his greying locks. He unquestionably receives a fair number of jokes on this subject.

Fifteen minutes is spent on applying the Polyfilla and 15 on concreting my hair into place. No breakfast is consumed as I am far too busy for food. A rummage through the wardrobe

Debra McArthur, 15, lives in Wallsend, on Tyneside, where she is in form 5R1 at Burnside High School. She and her 25 classmates were set 'A Life in the Day' as an assignment in personal writing – part of their English coursework for the new General Certificate of Secondary Education. Their teacher, Joan Sjovoll, thought the results were so good that she showed them to *The Sunday Times Magazine*. Debra hopes to take three A-levels before going on to university

finds my uniform and it's ready and set for action.

I usually enjoy school if I'm up to date with my schoolwork. I hate the feeling of being left behind with anything. I suppose I just hate missing out, even if avoiding this entails 'hard slog'. I enjoy school mainly because of the number of friends I have there. I also hate being alone. Another good reason for coming to school is to see my boyfriend, Craig, whom I meet every lunchtime. However, I do not let this interfere with my schoolwork. I believe that if I centre my full attention on either one or the other I will lose out somewhere.

At lunchtime I either go on a binge or I starve myself – never the happy medium. I usually starve for two reasons: either to make up for the binge which took place the previous day or to

save money. At Christmas I save every penny I receive in order to buy people decent gifts. When I do find I have quite a lot of money for myself it seems to affect my logic. I either give it away or buy other people things, instead of spending it on the one who earned it – me! But I do love having money to spend on myself. My father would say I waste it but I relish the thought of taking the chemist's counter by storm. It's unbelievable how quickly I can spend £20 on make-up and other such junk!

After school it's either netball practice for the school team or it's off home and tarting up time once again. I see Craig almost every evening. He says he doesn't mind what I look like but I like to feel as though I've made an effort for him. I either fit my homework in before I see him, during the time I see him,

or when he leaves for the bus at 11pm – which would account for the lateness in my morning getting-up time. Either way, my homework gets done.

I really enjoy looking after young children. They are so interesting. It was an ambition of mine to be a nanny or nursery nurse, but efforts to dissuade me eventually succeeded. 'You're too bright.' 'There's no money in it.' 'You'd get bored.' 'You'd be able to get a far better job.' I suppose I could babysit as a hobby until I have children of my own. I am looking forward very much to having children. Not actually the pregnancy and birth, but the end product. I am not keen on the idea of being a stereotypical mother/housewife. I also want a career, and a good one, but doing what? I wish I knew! My father continuously asks whether I have made up my mind yet. Now I am concentrating on gaining good exam results so that I will have a solid base from which to move in any direction – preferably upwards.

I often think about possible careers, pick them to pieces in my mind, discard the confused ideas and replace them with fantasies. I am a demon for fantasizing. I still maintain that I am going to be taken and made rich and famous due to an outstanding talent yet unrevealed (as you see in the movies). My bedtime thoughts consist of these two elements.

These are all factors which in later years will contribute to the steady increase of grey hairs. I usually wear my brain out at about 1am when I've worried myself silly and into slumberland. Peace at last!

Sunday Times

"I'm a bit of a keep-fit martial arts freak. I don't like lying thinking in the morning, so I get up fast at five or six o'clock and go for a run. When I have problems getting up, I start doing sit-ups while I'm still in bed. If I'm on tour I ask about gardens or some other place where I can run. In London I take my motorbike to Epping Forest. How far I go varies. During the week it's usually three to five miles. Weekends I'll run 10.

After my exercise and meditation, it's time for either a shower or a swim and a look at my diary. It's just an ordinary diary. I don't have a Filofax. Diaries are supposed to be small, kind of discreet things. I don't know how they got so big.

I'm a vegan, so at breakfast time I usually have a very small breakfast – plantain, avocado, tomatoes, and muesli with soya milk. I only ever drink fruit juice and water. I don't drink water from the tap. It's got to be mineral water. I really care about what goes into my body.

Clothes don't matter that much to me. I put on whatever is comfortable. Basically I think, what am I going to be doing today? Am I going to be walking, driving, am I going to be at home? I always wear something very light on my feet – usually martial arts shoes – and when I'm at home I spend a lot of time in tracksuits; or naked if I'm alone.

I don't really have a routine morning. I've got a finger in too many pies. I was touring last week, so a lot of time was spent gearing up for the evening performance. This week I've been in the recording studio. Next week I've really got to sit down and work on my plays. In between times I'm publishing books; I'm recording music; I'm acting – I've just finished playing a community police van driver in a film written by Alexei Sayle which stars Beryl Reid; I'm down at the wholefood co-op; I'm helping deal with people's problems at the housing co-op.

Up until a month ago a lot of my time was spent just co-ordinating things, but Tense, my manager, looks after that side of it now. I've got a place to work at home that's decked out like an office and I keep all my business – contracts or whatever – in it. If I'm working on a play I stay in there all day, maybe just coming out in the middle to do a bit more exercise. But when I'm doing poems it's completely different. Then I just take it easy and they come to me – it's inspired, really. I walk round the streets in the East End or Ladbroke Grove and the poems get written while I'm walking the streets.

Lunch is usually quite late on – about two or three o'clock, most days. I like to have one cooked meal with protein in it – beans, pulses, something like that. When I perform I like a nice empty stomach, so I eat a fairly heavy meal quite early and then I won't eat again.

I live alone with my mother. I find it hard to get into relationships and keep my work, so – I know this is going to sound a bit dodgy – when I need a feminine touch or someone to help out, instead of doing like most people and running and getting a girlfriend, I get my mother. She doesn't work for me or anything like that. We share the housework. If you see us together we act like two big kids. Wrestling all the time, and having farting competitions.

I've always dreamed of having a big family of my own. My mam had nine kids and raised a few others who were less fortunate than us, as well. I've always wanted nine kids, too. Lately I've been asking around – asking different girls if they'll have children for me. The thing is, I don't know how to do it. I'll have to ask an Indian guru, because some of them do. You see, I only want three pregnancies, but with three children each time.

I don't like to go to bed with a full stomach, so I only have a small evening meal. Sometimes I make a nut roast, or get some green bananas and boil those up.

I like to go to bed about 11, but when I get there depends on what's happening. For example, this week it's been two or three every morning. Usually I try and read before I go to sleep. Always something light – maybe on yoga or the martial arts. If I go to bed reading *State and Revolution*, I wake up in the morning with all the pressures of the world on my shoulders. After I turn the lights off, I assess the day that's gone past. I think how much good have I done today? I like to make sure I've done a good bit of good and then, just before that nodding-off period, I think about tomorrow.

Sunday Times

Benjamin Zephaniah, 28, was born in Handsworth, Birmingham. He came to London seven years ago, via Borstal and prison, and is now a successful performance poet and writer – but just missed being awarded a creative arts fellowship by Trinity College, Cambridge. He lives in the East End with his mother and their pet cat.

Writing about what typically or generally happens uses the present tense.

 Assignment 13 Write your own *Life In The Day Of* ....

Remember to:

- write in the present tense throughout your assignment,
- give an impression of all the different things that you do in and out of school, not just activities from any particular day.

or you could make up an imaginary *Life in the Day of* a famous person from history.

Special feature

On these pages are various articles and information about certain skills to enable you to research and then produce an extended piece of work called *Living in the 1990s*.

In addition to what is included here you may want to do your own background reading from various other sources.

Devising a questionnaire and using its results

Post-war drinkers join the wine set

By James Erlichman,
Consumer Affairs Correspondent

To celebrate its 40th year of polling people's habits, the Market Research Society unearthed what we all ate, drank, and wore in bed in 1946, and then asked the same questions for today.

Ration-starved Britain's favourite meal was tomato soup followed by Dover sole, roast chicken, and trifle.

Restaurant-chain thinking rules today. Prawn cocktail replaces the sole, steak and chips the chicken, and trifle has been relegated by Black Forest gateau.

Only 4 per cent said they drank wine with their meals in 1946. Today 61 per cent prefer wine.

Only 23 pollsters turned up at the society's inaugural meeting in 1946. Today the industry has 5,500 practitioners who charge fees of more than £200 million.

Women who agreed to be polled in 1946 revealed that they only owned one blouse and did 16.6 hours of housework a week. But they demurely failed to disclose anything about their sexual habits.

Today's women own 21 blouses, do half as much housework and reveal all about their sex lives.

The society commissioned 18 separate surveys to produce its report. More sober readers will discover that fears of serious economic recession loom larger now (52 per cent of respondents) than it did in Mr Attlee's day (32 per cent).

From *The Guardian*

1 Find out what all of these words mean before proceeding with the activities which follow.

relegated   pollsters   demurely

practitioners   disclose

2 In pairs make a list of the questions that must have been used to produce the information in this survey.
Example

```
What is your favourite meal in a restaurant?

First course:
Second course:
Third course:
```

3 Make up your own questionnaire to test the attitude of your friends and family to a much wider range of topics than food, drink and clothes. Investigate hobbies, money, TV, films, family life, education, etc. Add as many other areas to this list as possible. This will give you useful information about life now. If you can, use a computer to help you with this.

Typical teenager is TV addict, survey finds

THE TYPICAL British teenager is a clean, hardworking non-smoker, who spends generously on presents but is somewhat prone to headaches and ill-at-ease with the opposite sex, according to research published yesterday.

The teenage day starts with cereal, a glance at a popular newspaper and possibly a morning paper-round. It continues with regular attention to teeth and smelly armpits but an excessive intake of alcohol, sugar and fat; winds down with the minimum of homework and reading, and lots of goggling at television; and concludes with a bedtime between 10 and 11pm, after abortive attempts to extract information about sex from parents.

This picture emerges from a survey of 18,000 adolescents, who were questioned on a school day during term-time.

In all age groups (except girls aged 11 to 12), well over a third had done no homework the previous night, usually, they claimed, because it was not set. Even among fifth-year boys (15 to 16), only one in four spent more than an hour on their homework. Girls were more conscientious or maybe slower: more than one in three of the fifth-years did homework for more than an hour.

In all age groups, far more time is spent watching television. The majority of boys and girls watched television after school for at least two hours. 18 per cent of first-year boys (aged 11 to 12) watched for five hours or more. Remarkably, 20 per cent in this age group − and at least 15 per cent in the others − found further time to watch videos. One in three of the first-year boys also played computer games, although fewer than one in five of their girl classmates did so.

The majority of boys had not read at all the previous evening. One in four first-year girls, however, had spent at least an hour reading and, until the fourth year, the majority did some reading. But, for both sexes, the amount of reading tended to decline with age.

Barely 10 per cent in any age group had spent money on books in the previous month. The older boys and girls were four times more likely to spend money on alcohol and cigarettes.

The intake of alcohol − most commonly at home and so presumably with parental approval − is perhaps the most worrying aspect of the survey. Even among first-year girls, the lightest drinkers, one in three had had an alcoholic drink in the previous week.

Counting a pint of shandy as a unit of alcohol, the majority of first-year boys had consumed at least one unit, while one in three fifth-year boys and one in five girls had consumed more than seven. In the fifth-year, 7 per cent of the boys were already imbibing more than 21 units a week − the level at which adult men are warned that they may be in danger of alcoholism.

Smoking was slightly less of a problem. In all age groups, three in four had not smoked in the previous week and the majority had never started, or had smoked only one or twice. Most smoked lightly − even among fifth-year boys, under 6 per cent had smoked more than 66 cigarettes in the previous week.

The majority who did smoke already wanted to give up.

Other findings from the survey include:

● The majority bath or shower at least twice a week − about a quarter of fourth and fifth-year girls do so once a day.

● The majority think parents should be their main source of information about sex − but the majority also find this is not the case. About one in three fall back on friends for information, reluctantly in most cases.

● More than 95 per cent claim to help at home with gardening or housework. The majority of boys did so only sometimes but about 30 per cent of girls, against under 20 per cent of boys, helped every day. 29 per cent of first-year boys and 47 per cent of fifth-years had a paid term-time job.

from The Independent

Research statistics

Question 13. For how long did you watch television programmes (live or home-recorded) after school yesterday?
(Answers in %)

Boys years old	Not at all	Up to 1 h	1 + h	2 + h	3 + h	4 + h	5 + h
11–12	4.3	13.1	21.5	18.4	14.6	9.5	18.5
12–13	4.9	13.1	18.0	18.4	17.2	11.8	16.5
13–14	4.8	12.8	17.7	18.9	18.6	11.3	15.9
14–15	4.7	15.5	19.4	20.8	16.0	11.7	11.9
15–16	6.9	16.5	19.2	22.0	16.2	8.9	10.3

Girls years old	Not at all	Up to 1 h	1 + h	2 + h	3 + h	4 + h	5 + h
11–12	6.4	17.3	21.9	21.6	13.1	8.4	11.2
12–13	5.6	13.6	21.3	19.3	17.0	12.8	10.6
13–14	6.3	15.9	20.4	20.3	16.3	9.9	10.8
14–15	5.6	18.6	22.2	20.1	15.5	10.5	7.6
15–16	8.4	18.3	22.9	21.0	14.1	9.2	6.1

Question 15. How long did you spend playing computer games after school yesterday? (Answers in %)

Boys years old	Not at all	Up to 1 h	1+h	2+h	3+h	4+h	5+h
11–12	63.2	15.7	10.4	4.8	2.7	0.8	2.4
12–13	64.8	15.7	9.5	5.0	2.3	1.1	1.6
13–14	65.6	14.2	9.9	4.8	2.6	1.1	1.8
14–15	71.2	12.7	7.6	4.3	1.8	1.1	1.3
15–16	83.0	8.9	3.7	2.0	1.4	0.3	0.7

Girls years old	Not at all	Up to 1 h	1+h	2+h	3+h	4+h	5+h
11–12	83.1	10.3	4.2	1.4	0.8	0.2	0.0
12–13	86.5	8.6	3.0	1.3	0.3	0.1	0.2
13–14	89.4	6.8	2.3	0.9	0.4	0.0	0.1
14–15	91.4	5.7	1.8	0.7	0.3	0.1	0.1
15–16	95.5	3.4	0.8	0.3	0.0	0.0	

Question 16. How long did you spend doing homework after school yesterday? (Answers in %)

Boys years old	Not at all	Up to 1 h	1+h	2+h	3+h	4+h
11–12	36.2	43.7	15.9	3.4	0.6	0.2
12–13	50.7	34.1	12.0	1.8	0.8	0.6
13–14	46.8	31.7	16.4	3.7	1.0	0.3
14–15	43.3	29.3	19.6	5.8	1.2	0.9
15–16	60.3	14.6	13.9	7.2	2.9	1.2

Girls years old	Not at all	Up to 1 h	1+h	2+h	3+h	4+h
11–12	28.1	46.2	20.3	4.1	0.9	0.3
12–13	39.8	37.1	18.3	4.2	0.6	0.1
13–14	37.2	30.8	21.8	7.1	2.3	0.9
14–15	35.3	29.2	24.1	8.7	2.2	0.5
15–16	54.6	14.0	15.9	10.7	3.3	1.5

Question 19d. How many hours did you work for money last week? (Answers in %)

Boys years old	0	1	2	3	4	5	6–7	8–10	11–20	21+
11–12	79.3	4.9	5.1	2.8	2.6	1.1	1.8	1.2	1.0	0.2
12–13	56.2	4.7	5.4	3.4	3.0	1.8	4.4	18.2	2.5	0.5
13–14	57.6	3.8	6.4	5.8	4.9	4.1	7.5	6.6	2.9	0.5
14–15	45.1	3.6	5.7	5.3	5.3	3.9	8.3	16.2	5.7	1.0
15–16	54.1	1.8	3.2	4.1	4.0	4.0	6.7	12.5	7.8	1.9

Girls years old	0	1	2	3	4	5	6–7	8–10	11–20	21+
11–12	86.1	3.6	3.9	1.4	1.5	0.6	1.5	1.0	0.3	0.2
12–13	65.2	3.8	4.7	3.6	2.8	1.4	1.8	15.5	1.2	0.1
13–14	70.0	3.4	4.1	3.7	3.2	2.3	4.0	6.7	2.2	0.3
14–15	49.6	2.0	3.4	4.7	4.7	3.5	7.6	19.7	4.4	0.5
15–16	51.0	0.9	2.3	3.2	5.0	3.5	8.7	14.7	8.3	2.5

Question 44. With respect to smoking, which of the following most nearly describes you? (Answers in %)

Boys years old	Never started	Once or twice	Given up	Like to stop	Not want to stop
11–12	75.8	16.8	5.3	1.4	0.8
12–13	62.1	23.7	10.5	2.4	1.3
13–14	49.3	27.8	11.9	7.6	3.4
14–15	41.5	28.4	13.5	10.8	5.9
15–16	37.8	27.3	13.5	14.6	6.9

Girls years old	Never started	Once or twice	Given up	Like to stop	Not want to stop
11–12	80.1	13.9	4.9	0.9	0.2
12–13	59.8	23.6	11.4	3.9	1.2
13–14	44.9	26.0	16.1	11.0	2.9
14–15	32.4	25.4	18.8	16.8	6.6
15–16	33.5	24.2	18.6	16.8	6.9

In groups, look at these photographs. Do they confirm the impression of teenagers given in the article?

▼ Assignment 14

This assignment is about living in the 1990s.

Stage 1
▼
Decide on the precise focus that your assignment is going to have. For example, is it going to look at teenage life, family life, society in general?

Stage 2
▼
Agree how you are going to research your article. The chart below shows some possible methods.

Stage 3
▼
Plan and organize your work. You could make a checklist of all the stages of your research.

Stage 4
▼
Decide who your writing is aimed at, for example, your friends at school, readers of a national paper, readers of a teenage magazine. (This may involve some research.) Decide what the purpose of your piece will be, for example, to show that times are changing or that young people are very responsible now!

Stage 5
▼
Complete your draft assignment by including statistical information, photographs, if possible, anecdotes or any other form of evidence that you can find.

Stage 6
▼
Produce your final draft. (You could type it and make a class pamphlet or book containing all the articles you have produced.)

Key words

subject detail attitude	report feature past
research quotation	present tense
observation statistics	questionnaire
	statement third person

Key techniques

- using third person and past tense for reports (for example, *She was* sleeping in the open air.)
- using detail to make reports/features more vivid
- using quotations to bring out your subject's voice
- selecting significant events in reports/features
- using interviews to produce features
- using questionnaires
- interpreting basic statistics
- researching a feature/report
- presenting points of view

UNIT 5 *Publicity material*

Pamphlets or publicity leaflets provide information and opinion in a particular kind of style.

Publicity leaflets

1 Study the page opposite from a leaflet produced by The Children's Legal Centre called *At what age can I?*

2 Make a list of any information here which you find interesting or which you don't understand.

3 Talk about any of these 'rights' which you find surprising or contradictory. As far as you know, is anything listed now factually incorrect?

4 In groups make a list of all the rights that you think you have at the age of sixteen. In particular, consider travel, home, sex, work, alcohol, the law. Find out more about these.

5 In 1959 the United Nations issued a *Declaration of the rights of children*. It included comments on education, food, medical care, love, protection from discrimination. In groups, draw up a list of the ten most important rights you think all young people should have. Agree two or three practical methods of ensuring all young people have these rights. For example, if you believe that children should have a say in the way their country is run, you might want to suggest that the age at which people can vote should be lowered . . . to what age?

 Assignment 15

Design a leaflet showing your 'rights' in either your family or at your school at age 14/15/16.

Example

14	*at school*
	All students can choose which subject to study

15	*at home*
	You can stay out until 10.00pm during the week

Design the leaflet carefully to put over your beliefs clearly to people of your *own* age. You might choose to illustrate it and to use a different shape or layout from *At what age can I?*

17

You can be sent to prison if you are convicted of a serious offence (section 19(1) Powers of Criminal Courts Act 1973).

A probation order can be made on you (section 2 Powers of Criminal Courts Act 1973).

A care order can no longer be made on you, nor can you be received into care (sections 1 and 70(1) CYPA 1969; section 2 Child Care Act 1980).

You can hold a licence to drive most vehicles apart from heavy goods vehicles (section 96 Road Traffic Act 1972).

You can buy or hire any firearm or ammunition (section 21 Firearms Act 1968).

You can have an air weapon with you in a public place (section 22 Firearms Act 1968).

You can become a street trader (section 20 CYPA 1933 as amended by section 35 CYPA 1963).

A girl can join the armed forces with parental consent at 17½.

You can apply for a helicopter pilot's licence (schedule 9 Air Navigation Order 1980).

You can hold a pilot's licence (Air Navigation Order 1972 SI 1972 No 129 article 20).

18

You reach the age of majority – you are an adult in the eyes of the law (section 1 Family Law Reform Act 1969).

You can vote in general and local elections (section 1(1)(c), 24(1) and schedule 2 Representation of the People Act 1949).

You can serve on a jury (section 7(2)(a) Juries Act 1974).

You have complete contractual capacity so you can own land, buy a house or flat, apply for a mortgage, sue and be sued in your own right and you can act as an executor or administrator of a deceased person's estate.

You can open a bank account or a Post Office Girobank account without a parent's signature.

You can apply for a passport without a parent's consent.

You can change your name (rule 92(8) Matrimonial Causes Rules 1977 SI No 344; Enrolment of Deeds (Change of Name) (Amendment) Regulations 1969 SI No 1432). If you are over 16 but under 18 you can only change your name with the written consent of your parent(s).

You can make a will (section 7 Wills Act 1837 as amended by section 3 Family Law Reform Act 1969). If you're in the armed forces or a marine or a seaman you can make a will under the age of 18 (section 1 Wills (Soliders and Sailors) Act 1918 as amended by section 3 Family Law Reform Act 1969).

You can make an application for legal aid in your own right. Under 18s will normally need an adult to do so on their behalf (section 7(5) Legal Aid Act 1974).

You can be represented directly by a solicitor rather than through an intermediary in High Court or county court civil proceedings. But if you are under 18 and wish to sue in the county court for money owed to you, you can be represented directly through a solicitor (rule 2 Rules of the Supreme Court Order 80; section 80 County Courts Act 1959).

You can no longer be made a ward of court.

You can buy and drink alcohol in a bar (section 169(2) Licensing Act 1964).

You can hold a licence to drive a medium-sized goods vehicle (maximum 7.5 tonnes) (section 96 Road Traffic Act 1972).

You can enter a betting shop and place a bet; you can also work in one (section 21 Betting, Gaming and Lotteries Act 1963). You can enter a bingo club under the age of 18 as long as you don't take part in a game (section 21 Gaming Act 1968).

If you are adopted, you can see your birth certificate on application to the Registrar General (section 51 Adoption Act 1976).

You can take part in an acting, dancing or singing performance abroad without a licence (section 42 CYPA 1963).

You can be tattooed (section 1 Tattooing of Minors Act 1969)

You can join the armed forces without parental consent.

You can take part in an exhibition or performance of hypnotism (section 3 Hypnotism Act 1952 as amended by Family Law Reform Act 1969).

You can donate your body to science or anatomical study or donate your body organs without parental permission.

You have to pay for dental treatment unless you are still in full-time education, or pregnant, or certain other circumstances apply (Leaflet D 11/ April 1984, DHSS).

You can see a category 18 film (British Board of Film Censors categories, approved by the Home Office and accepted by local authorities). You can buy a video given a certificate for viewing by adults only. Certificates will state a video is suitable for viewing by children of a specified age (Video Recordings Act 1984).

You can pawn an article at a pawnshop (section 114(2) Consumer Credit Act 1974 as enacted by Commencement No 8 Order SI 1551 1983).

19

All young people are entitled to full-time education, up to the age of 19 either at school or college (section 8(b) and section 114 Education Act 1944).

21

A man may consent to a 'homosexual act' in private if he and his partner are both over 21 (section 1 Sexual Offences Act 1967).

You can become a MP or local councillor (section 1(1)(c); section 24(1) and schedule 2 Representation of the People Act 1949).

You can hold a licence to drive a large passenger vehicle or heavy goods vehicle (section 96 Road Traffic Act 1972).

You can apply for a licence to sell alcohol (section 98 Licensing Act 1964)

The Children's Legal Centre runs a free advice service on all aspects of law affecting children and young people in England and Wales, by letter or telephone (2pm to 5pm weekdays – 01 359 6251).

Leaflets are an effective means of informing the public about potential dangers to life.

Design

Study this pamphlet carefully. It is printed over two pages but was originally on A4-sized paper folded twice as indicated below.

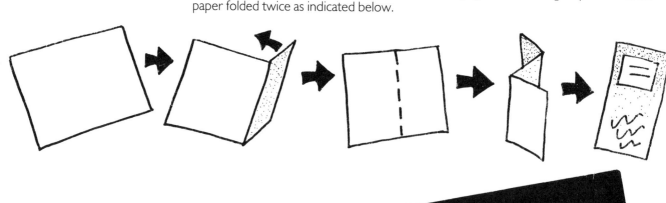

In an emergency

! Don't panic. It's important that you remain calm.

! Remove any glue or solvents and make sure that your child gets plenty of fresh air.

! If the child is drowsy or unconscious lie the child on his or her side.

! Make sure someone stays near so that if the child is sick, he or she can be prevented from inhaling vomit. When the child awakens be reassuring; he or she is likely to be confused and upset.

! If the child is unconscious contact a family doctor immediately. If the doctor is not available, dial 999 and ask for an ambulance.

! After the emergency, give your child the opportunity to talk about the incident and about any other worries he or she may have.

IF YOU NEED FURTHER HELP CONTACT:

WHAT TO DO ABOUT GLUE-SNIFFING

Advice for parents on the misuse of glue and other solvents

HEALTH EDUCATION COUNCIL
78 New Oxford Street London WC1A 1AH

M50

Tanbryn Ltd 750m 5/85

1 In groups, decide:
- how this leaflet has been organized,
- what use has been made of headings, lists, signs, artwork,
- how effective you think the leaflet is as a piece of communication aimed at parents.

2 In groups, use the information in the pamphlet to help you invent two short scenes: one in which child glue-sniffers are helped by a sympathetic adult, the other in which parent(s) and child(ren) handle the situation badly.

What is glue-sniffing?

Glue-sniffing means breathing in the vapours given off by certain types of glue in order to get intoxicated or 'high', rather like getting drunk on alcohol. The ingredient that causes this effect is the solvent contained in many brands of glue as well as many other household and industrial products.

Why do youngsters sniff glue?

The reasons why young people glue-sniff vary with each individual. Usually it's out of curiosity. Some kids do it because they want to belong to a group where sniffing happens to be part of the group's activities.

Sniffing is also a cheap and easy substitute for alcohol, especially when you are under-age. Some kids may be unhappy for a number of possible reasons and may try sniffing either to seek attention or to escape from their problems.

For most youngsters it is a passing phase, but for some it can become a dangerous habit.

What are the dangers?

By inhaling poisonous vapours, people put themselves at risk of:

△ Accidents which can happen more easily when someone is intoxicated.

△ Suffocation.

△ Possible physical and psychological damage in the long term. (Some youngsters have died as a direct or indirect result of sniffing glue or other solvents.)

What are the signs?

The most obvious signs that a youngster might be a sniffer are:

○ A chemical smell on the breath or unexplained traces of glue or other solvents found either on the body or on clothes.

○ A sudden unexplained interest in glue, nail varnish or other solvent-based products.

A combination of the following could also be an indication of sniffing:

○ Unusual soreness or redness around the mouth, nose or eyes.

○ Persistent, irritable cough.

○ Slurred speech.

○ Sudden irritable or moody behaviour combined perhaps with secrecy about movements.

○ A sudden and uncharacteristic decline in school performance possibly combined with the start of truancy.

What you can do

Children are often curious and like to experiment with the latest craze. If you feel that your child may be mixing with youngsters who sniff solvents, you could talk to your child and warn him or her of the possible risks and dangers involved. Remember don't 'jump in' without thinking carefully about how you are going to handle the situation.

Children sometimes take to sniffing out of boredom. Encourage your child to get involved in enjoyable activities such as youth clubs, sports and games and support your child's ventures in these and similar pursuits.

Your interest and support are important to your children. Encourage them to talk to you about any worries or problems they may have.

Teach your children to use household products only for their proper purposes.

Teach them to follow any labelling instructions about safety.

And check up on any unusual use of glue, nail varnish or other solvent-based products.

3 Pick out the significant points from these two views of experiments on animals. The first is part of a leaflet produced by the Research Defence Society. The second is a page advertisement carried by the Animal Rights Magazine *Turning Point*. Which do you think makes the more powerful case and why?

Are animal experiments necessary for cosmetic products?

● It is very easy to apply double standards and the issue of animal experiments required by the cosmetics industry is a good example.

● Few people are prepared to suffer damage to their skin, hair, eyes or mouth because soap, shampoo or toothpaste has not been properly tested before being offered for sale.

● Few mothers are prepared to place their children at an unknown risk as a result of swallowing skin preparations.

● Few people would refrain from suing a manufacturer whose products disfigured or seriously damaged them in normal use.

● To ensure safety in use, animal testing is unavoidable for the cosmetics industry at the present time.

However, we must ensure that those animals that do HAVE to be used are properly safeguarded.

The facts

Cosmetics and toiletries are used by a very large proportion of the population and they include soaps, toothpaste, shampoos, eye preparations, creams of various kinds, mouthwashes, hair colourants, lipsticks and baby powders. These are applied to the skin, to the eyes, to the hair or to the mouth, which are sensitive areas. Most of the preparations are made from ingredients whose purity and safety characteristics are known, and in nearly all cases these ingredients have been tested on animals. In the past, many dangerous ingredients including alkaloids, belladonna, compounds of arsenic and toxic dyes were included in various products and the only means of testing whether these products were safe was by trial and error. The result of such a system was serious injury in many cases and even death. Today such problems are non-existent. Complaints now are from people who are particularly sensitive and unable to use products which are perfectly satisfactory to the vast majority of the population.

In conclusion, it may be said that the cosmetic and toiletries products have an excellent safety record due to thorough consumer product testing—at the present time animals are a small but very necessary part of this.

THE LAW STILL ALLOWS PEOPLE TO SQUIRT WEEDKILLER IN A BABY'S EYES, INJECT IT WITH POISON, GROW CANCERS ON ITS BACK, BURN ITS SKIN OFF, EXPOSE IT TO RADIATION AND EVENTUALLY KILL IT, IN UNRELIABLE EXPERIMENTS.

SO LONG AS IT'S ONLY AN ANIMAL.

We can prove that experiments on animals are as misleading and unproductive as they are inhuman and sickeningly cruel.

Indeed, important life saving medical advances such as blood transfusions have actually been delayed for many years by such experiments.

So write to us now for the evidence. It might make you feel sick. But it'll also make you want to help.

Name

Address

Please post to: National Anti-Vivisection Society Ltd, 51 Harley Street, London W1N 1DD.

NATIONAL ANTI-VIVISECTION SOCIETY

 **Assignment 16** Design a pamphlet or advertisement for a cause about which you have strong views, for example, women's rights, nuclear power, AIDS.
Include on a separate sheet of paper your own notes under the following headings:

Why this issue is important

Who the leaflet is aimed at

The important messages to communicate about my issue are ...

Some leaflets deliberately adopt a different style of presentation to appeal to their intended readers.

Styles of presentation

Read this leaflet through carefully. It originally appeared on two sides of A4 paper.
In groups, agree:
- who it is aimed at,
- why this style has been chosen,
- what your learn about the Samaritans from this.

Assignment 17   Produce some publicity material for an organization of your own choice using this technique. Include photographs or artwork as well as captions, dialogue and information.

You could set up the photographs yourself or adapt photographs from magazines. Choose a caring organization; for example, Childline, Citizens' Advice Bureaux, a local Hospital, your tutor . . .

Mounting a publicity campaign

Before attempting this assignment study these guidelines from *How to Complain* by B. Avison.

General guidelines for organizers

■ Hold a preliminary meeting to be attended by people who have responded to the suggestion of group action and indicated a willingness to get involved. Give everyone an opportunity to express his/her views. Consider electing a committee which would be responsible for the day-to-day organization of effort needed to carry out the wishes of the group.

■ Prepare a statement that briefly sets out your group's aim, the reasons for the complaint and, if possible, the time in which you reasonably expect something to be done about it. This is a good way of discovering any basic differences of opinion or uncertainty about the issues involved that should be tackled at this early stage; and you'll also end up with a useful summary of your group's intentions.

■ Take steps to find out who is *really* responsible for putting matters right and consider how best to approach them.

■ Before taking any action, find out whether there are any legal restrictions you should observe so that you don't unwittingly lay yourselves open to being sued or prosecuted.

■ Remember that publicity can be one of your most effective weapons, both in drumming up wider support or raising funds and in forcing the responsible person or authorities to react.

■ Seek support from people who can influence public opinion and whose social standing or relevant qualifications command respect. This makes it much more difficult for the other side to dismiss your group as a bunch of politically-motivated extremists.

■ A petition is likely to have real impact only if you can get either 100 per cent support from those affected (for example, all the parents of children attending a school threatened with closure) or a really impressive number of signatures; otherwise, the time it takes would be better spent on other campaign work. If you do organize a petition, it should carry a simple statement of your request at the top, preceded by the words, 'We, the undersigned, ask [the title of the person being petitioned]'. People should give their addresses and occupations as well as their signatures. You can collect signatures in the street, but take care: you may risk being had up for obstructing the highway. When you present the petition, turn it into a publicity event by inviting the local press and getting someone well-known to deliver or accept it (for example, a petition to the Secretary of State for Education could be accepted at the House of Commons by your MP).

■ There are two sides to any argument. You'll have a better chance of winning it if you find out what the other side is likely to say, both in its own support and to undermine your case. You can then prepare yourselves with relevant evidence to support a counter-argument.

Publicizing your cause

■ The purpose of publicity is to present your case clearly and convincingly to the people whose support can help you to win. It is *not* true that all publicity is good publicity; careful thought and meticulous planning are needed when selecting which methods to use. Whenever possible, you should avoid causing inconvenience other than to those responsible for provoking your complaint, or you risk alienating potential supporters.

PUBLIC MEETINGS

A number of factors affect the success of a public meeting.

■ The venue: find somewhere pleasant, convenient to reach, just large enough for the number of people you expect, with adequate seating and any other facilities you require.

■ The agenda: the meeting may attract more people if, in addition to the two key components of speeches and the answering of questions, it offers a degree of entertainment – a film or slide-show, for example, or a drinks party afterwards.

■ The speakers: choose effective speakers and, if possible, get someone well-known to address the meeting in support of your cause – your MP, perhaps, or a local celebrity. Speeches should be kept brief, and the audience given every opportunity to ask questions and so get involved.

■ The audience: for a public meeting to be a success, it must be well attended by the people at whom it is aimed. This means advertising it in advance, for example, in the local press and on leaflets and posters; it also means fixing the meeting for a day and time that will be most convenient for the intended audience, and even taking into consideration rival attractions such as television programmes.

■ The publicity: invite the local press (from radio and television as well as newspapers). If they don't attend, write your own report of the meeting in the form of a brief article and get it round to the editors the next day; newspapers may be able to use an illustration, for example, a photograph of the main speaker.

■ Real-life examples of how the circumstances of your group's complaint are affecting people's lives are more likely to attract the media's attention and the public's sympathy than just an abstract discussion of the principles and policies involved.

PAMPHLETS AND POSTERS

Although the media constitute a useful publicity tool, you cannot control their coverage of your case in either quality or quantity, and so you may consider producing your own printed material, in the form of leaflets, news sheets or posters. Such material requires careful thought, particularly about its design. Whether you distribute it in the streets or through people's letter-boxes or display it on notice-boards or hoardings, it will be jostling for attention with all the other printed matter around. A powerful photograph can help, as well as a clever use of typefaces and layout. Don't try to cram in too much information; it is better to be brief and simple, making it clear how the reader can find out more or join your campaign.

As far as the law is concerned, you can distribute or sell printed materials such as leaflets in the street as long as you don't cause an obstruction. Posters can be stuck up in public places if they are an advertisement for a political, social, educational or religious meeting if they are no larger than six feet square, and if they don't obstruct the highway (check with your Town Hall that they don't have any additional bye-laws you should observe). You are not allowed to stick up posters on private property without the owner's permission (by doing so, you risk a hefty fine).

Assignment 18   The situation

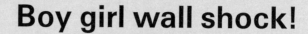

Boy girl wall shock!

It has been decided by your Local Education Authority that coeducation is to cease immediately. According to educational research it has been 'proved' that girls learn better if taught with girls by women and that the same need for single-sex education applies for boys.

Accordingly the following action has been agreed.

- All coeducational schools will be divided into two separate institutions by means of a large wall.

- Arrangements for sharing of certain facilities, for example, sports halls, swimming pools, secretarial services, will be made where necessary.

- Essential building work will be carried out over the summer holidays to ensure separate entrances to all sites and amenities.

- All teachers in schools which are currently single-sex must be deployed or redeployed according to gender; teachers from coeducational schools will teach in the appropriate new school.

The campaign

Stage 1 In groups, decide on your response to this, that is, whether you agree or disagree with it. Prepare a statement that briefly sets out your aims.

Stage 2 Decide who you will have to approach in order to put matters right (or support this initiative).

Stage 3 Produce a petition.

Stage 4 Make a list of the arguments likely to be used against your campaign and your answers to them.

Stage 5 Plan a public meeting.
(Before going any further you should divide up the jobs that need to be done and allocate them to members of your group.)
Decide on a venue.
Produce an agenda.
Choose some local speakers and write to them to invite them to take part.

Stage 6 Produce an attractive poster with a campaign slogan. Produce an informative leaflet.

Stage 7   Develop this situation so that you can explore the issues as fully as possible.
You might like to stage a public meeting or demonstration, recorded on audio or
video-tape, in which members of your class play different roles.
NB Each member of the group should keep a full record of their campaign for this
assignment, including:

1. their own notes of her/his group's decisions,

2. notes describing jobs undertaken,

3. pamphlets, letters, leaflets, agendas, petitions and any other forms of publicity produced,

4. a report for a local newspaper of your public meeting.

Key words

pamphlet leaflet   opinion petition
information audience   agenda

Key techniques

● designing a suitable layout
● organizing information and researching evidence
● using vocabulary suitable for your intended reader
● choosing appropriate styles
● developing an original style of presentation

UNIT 6 *The natural world*

Presenting issues related to our natural world is an important style of writing found in newspapers, magazines and books of general interest.

Read this article from *The New Scientist* in which Colin Shawyer and Peter Banks ask why the white owl and the barn owl are now so close to becoming extinct.

FOR CENTURIES the barn owl, *Tyto alba*, has lived alongside the farmer. The farmer's activities largely dictated the number of owls, and a flourishing population of owls was a sign of the quality of the wildlife of British farmlands. Just how many owls there used to be is a matter for speculation. Historical writings are the only means by which we can judge the size of the population in the past. Chroniclers of the late 1700s were unanimous that the white owl was very common throughout England, Wales, Ireland and southern Scotland, inhabiting almost every parish. A single farm building might shelter several small breeding communities. Such high densities are difficult to comprehend today.

Until the beginning of the 19th century the barn owl prospered, benefiting greatly from the enclosure of land. Many new farmsteads sprang up at this time. These, together with the increasing network of field boundaries, provided a wealth of new grassland – the ideal habitat for small mammals and rich hunting grounds for the owl.

The owls' prosperity did not last. Since 1800, the species has had a chequered history. About 1820, the owl seemed to go into decline. The rapid reduction in the number of owls coincided with the spread of game rearing and the associated explosion in the number of gamekeepers. Pole traps, steel jaws set at flying height, and the newly invented breech-loading gun accounted for most of the owls killed. At the same time, the middle-class vogue for taxidermy took its toll. The beautiful heart-faced barn own graced many a Victorian parlour. By 1860, persecution approached its peak. The number of barn owls continued to fall.

Towards the end of the 19th century, things began to look up for the owl. The public grew more aware of the benefits of the owl as a killer of rodents. New laws banned the use of pole traps; and the climate in winter improved. The improvement continued throughout the First World War, when many keepers were called to the colours, reducing the level of human persecution of owls.

The end of the war saw a resurgence of gamekeeping, and the population of owls began to decline once more. In 1932, George Blaker conducted a national survey of barn owls. He reported a population of 12 000 pairs in England and Wales. Blaker's survey provided a baseline against which future surveyors could assess changes in the owl's status.

The winter of 1940 was a milestone in the barn owl's history. Heavy snow blanketed the country. Owls hunting over the frozen fields had difficulty finding food. But in the rickyard, thousands of rodents scurried back and forth. Flocks of finches fed on split corn. Food was plentiful for the owl. All this was about to change. That year the snow lay longer on the ground than in any year since the 19th century. Yet worse was still to come; for this marked the start of a progressive and severe worsening of the winter climate. The farmyard was to change too. With the coming of the combine harvester and the disappearance of the working horse in the mid-1940s, rickyards and fodder stores began to disappear, together with the rats and mice they supported.

In the absence of the farmyard's guaranteed supply of food, snowfall became increasingly important to a species living at the northern limit of its range. When we analysed the climatic records and figures for the changing number of owls, we found that the critical factor for the success or failure of the owl appears to be the number of days on which snow covers the ground. The small mammals on which the owl relies for food retreat beneath the snow, where they are invisible to the hunting owl. The sudden reduction in the food supply at a crucial time of year prevents the owl from building up reserves ready for the coming breeding season. Birds that are not in a fit condition often raise smaller broods. However, there is little evidence that cold weather itself kills the birds except when the winter is exceptionally hard, as in 1963, or for those birds occupying marginal habitat on high ground.

The weather becomes critical for the owl when snow lies for 20 days or longer in any one winter. This has consistently produced a population crash. We found that since 1932 the barn owls' numbers have fluctuated rhythmically in a cycle averaging 3·4 years. The low points of the cycle correspond with those years of maximum snow cover. These cycles also seem to be in line with those of the short-tailed vole, the owls' favourite prey on mainland Britain.

Britain's winter weather remained remarkably mild between 1900 and 1939. On average, snow lay on the ground for 12 days; only in 1917, when there was snow for 29 days, was the ground covered for longer than the critical period. In the 47 years between 1940 and 1986, snow cover reached or exceeded the critical period in 22 winters. In nine of them, snow lay for more than 30 days. The figures for the very severe winters of 1947, 1963 and 1979 were 46, 63 and 51 days. From 1940 the number of days of snow cover each year increased progressively and dramatically.

Heavy and continuous rain is another hazard for the barn owl. The birds' feathers quickly become waterlogged making it difficult for owls to hunt in wet weather. This can be critical in the breeding season, from the time the egg is fertilized to the time when the young fledge leaves the nest. We assessed the effects of rainfall throughout this period, which lasts from May to September, between 1900 and 1986. We took 140 per cent of the average rainfall as the critical point after which the rain begins to prevent the birds from feeding properly. This is the figure the Meteorological Office uses to define excess rainfall. According to this definition, 1946 and 1958 were the most recent years when rain was exceptionally heavy in the summer. In 1958, the owl population fell to an all-time low.

Drought also exacts a penalty from barn owls. Although it does not stop the owl from hunting, it can reduce the number of small mammals. The population of owls fell noticeably in the breeding seasons following the droughts of 1949 and 1976.

All three climatic extremes – persistent snow, heavy rain and drought – threaten the barn owl in the short term. When these bad years are part of a generally worsening trend in climate they become responsible for the long-term decline.

In 1982, we began another survey of the barn owl – the first for 50 years. After three years we had received more than 11 000 records from farmers, naturalists and the general public. The results charted the continuing decline of the owl, where its strongholds are, and revealed what, apart from the weather, was killing the owls.

Barn owls usually nest in buildings, in holes in trees or in rock fissures. Trees and buildings are the commonest sites; less than 2 per cent of our records reported nests in rock fissures. What is remarkable is the geographical variation in the proportions of different types of nest site. We found 69 per cent of nest sites were in artificial structures, and 29 per cent were in trees, but there is enormous variation from one region to another. In Devon, only 5 per cent of barn owls nest in trees, while in Suffolk the proportion rises to 70 per cent. Simple opportunism, nesting wherever there is a suitable site, seems to play little part in governing the bird's choice. Rainfall is the decisive factor. We found a definite East-West division, with barn owls in the wetter western counties favouring nest sites in buildings. Those in the drier east of the country are more likely to nest in trees. All barn owls are prone to waterlogging; but young, inexperienced birds are especially vulnerable. The advantage of nesting in a barn, for example, is obvious. The young bird can learn to fly in a dry environment and might even start to learn to hunt if there is prey available. An owl may prefer a particular type of nest but the choice is increasingly limited. Farmers have no use for old buildings, decaying workers' cottages or disused animal houses. Such sites are disappearing. Old trees, large enough to house owls, are also in short supply. The shortage of nest sites does not pose a problem yet because there are not enough owls to fill them. But the owls' recovery could eventually falter, for lack of places to nest.

The barn owl suffers substantial losses each year, although the causes of death have changed with the times. Between 1982 and 1986 the average number of young a pair of owls fledged was 3·35 in England and Wales and 2·84 in Scotland. Our calculations suggest that more than 10 000 birds must die each year. We based our analysis on a sample of 764 records from the survey. By far the greatest cause of death was road accidents, which accounted for 52 per cent of all records – the equivalent of 5000 deaths a year. We must treat these alarming figures with some caution, as many of these birds might have died of natural causes if traffic had not killed them first. Put into a historical context, road accidents might, nevertheless, account for the same proportion of deaths as gamekeepers and taxidermists a century ago.

Drowning, at 6 per cent, is the second most common cause of death. This in itself is remarkable, but more so because almost all drowned owls are female. Moreover, most birds drown in July. This is the time when female birds leave the nest for the first time after some eight weeks of continuous incubation and brooding. The birds need to clean themselves and rid the plumage of parasites. The deaths we recorded all seem to be the result of unsuccessful bathing.

Chemicals are a more insidious threat to the barn owl. While the chlorinated hydrocarbon pesticides such as DDT and dieldrin poisoned many birds of prey from the 1950s onward, there was much less evidence that the barn owl suffered substantially. The greater threat now is that owls might eat rodents poisoned with anticoagulant rodenticides – especially those second-generation poisons that are replacing warfarin as rats grow resistant to it. Although poisoning is not a common cause of death (3·2 per cent of all deaths) it can tip the balance in those communities that have already reached a critically low level.

The barn owls' decline in the past 50 years is most apparent in the colder regions of eastern and northern Britain and, more locally, on high ground where the snow stays longer. Indeed, 85 per cent of Britain's barn owls breed in the warmer, more sheltered river valleys below 100 metres. But existing strongholds on estates managed in the traditional way are vulnerable, threatened by their isolation. As other farms are worked intensively, the grassland links along rivers and hedgerows are lost.

Today, the population in Britain and Ireland is about 5200 pairs. In England and Wales the population has declined from 12 000 pairs 50 years ago to 3800 pairs now. Throughout northwest Europe and North America, in regions where the winter temperatures average less than 3·5°C, the owl has also waned, in many cases more severely than in Britain – but probably for all the same reasons.

Our survey shows that the barn owl can live alongside modern farming and commercial forestry if rough grassland links are maintained between neighbouring communities of owls. In many parts of the fenlands of East Anglia, for example, on some of Britain's most intensively farmed land, there are often more barn owls than in the more traditionally farmed regions of Devon. In Lincolnshire, the narrow strips of grassland along rivers and drainage ditches provide a good supply of food and a network of corridors rich in prey along which young birds can disperse. Efforts to conserve the barn owl must concentrate on protecting habitats within existing strongholds. We must follow this with a scheme to recreate, throughout the country, grassland strips 6 to 10 metres wide, along rivers and the headlands around fields. Such corridors will re-establish continuity between these strongholds.

The Hawk Trust has established two schemes to forge such links. The Farmland Link, a network of grasslands along streams and around the edges of fields, has begun on five farms in Buckinghamshire. The Riverside Link aims to create similar corridors along waterways. In Lincolnshire, the Anglian Water Authority has already introduced some conservation measures and is following the Hawk Trust's plans for river corridors.

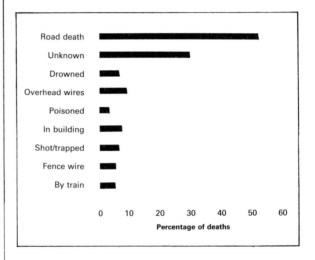

It is harder to counteract the effects of severe winter weather. Farmers and landowners can provide dumps of winter grain in hedgerows and isolated barns to attract small mammals to places where they know barn owls forage. Food dumps can be only a short-term measure but they give the owls a breathing space and might help birds to reach good condition in time for the breeding season. Supplementary feeding at wild sites during winter encourages owls to produce large and sometimes second broods. Owls at neighbouring sites that do not have access to extra food may fail to breed.

A more controversial measure is to reintroduce owls bred in captivity to old haunts. The practice is widespread, involving about 2000 birds a year. But without careful management and creation of suitable habitats for the released birds, the owls often fail to breed for the same reason as their wild counterparts.

The barn owls' future is beginning to look a little brighter. If, as conservationists and farmers suggest, Britain no longer needs to farm all its arable land, we should be in a better position to protect and enlarge the owls' existing refuges and recreate the grassland links between them. Surplus farmland, however, will not benefit the owl – or any other wildlife – if no one coordinates the plans for managing the pockets of land, or if they fail to take into account the barn owls' special need for rough linear grassland. The barn owls' reprieve also depends on the incentives the government provides to farmers to create wide headlands around fields. Many farmers regard themselves as 'custodians of the barn owl' and express a wish to farm not only for food but also for the owl. With that sort of commitment, perhaps the white owl has a chance of survival.

1 Copy this chart and, in pairs, fill in next to the dates the numbers of owls. The first entry has been completed for you.

Numbers of owls

1780–1800	Evidence of many white owls in Britain. At least one per parish.
1800–1820	
1820–1860	
1860–1918	
1918–1932	
1932–1940	
1940–1982	
1982–1986	

2 In pairs, using the chart and the information given in the article, decide whether these statements about the ways in which white owls die are true or false or whether you do not have enough information to be certain.
   a) All white owl deaths are caused by human beings.
   b) Male owls drown the females.
   c) Drowning is the second most common cause of death .
   d) We know how all white owls die.
   e) If there were no motor-vehicles the owls would not be in danger.
   f) Owls killed on the roads would be killed in the same year by some other means anyway.
   g) Human beings could take certain actions to improve the chances of owls surviving.
   h) Most unexplained deaths are caused by owls dying during bad weather.
   i) The owl is a pest and should be shot.
   j) The owl is a positive benefit to the natural world.

3 In pairs, talk about how the inclusion of pictures and a chart helps to put over the writer's message.

4 In pairs make three lists under these headings of anything in this piece of writing that you would describe as 'scientific' or 'mathematical' or 'historical'. Why is such information necessary in this style of writing?

Writing about environmental issues for a wider audience involves using a combination of scientific information and persuasive argument. In order to warn about the future it often contains references to the past.

▼Assignment 19

Using the information on these two pages and your own research produce an article of about 4–6 sides of A4 paper suitable for a general interest teenage magazine.

Stage 1 Study these two pages and consider how any material contained here would have to be adapted for your particular audience.

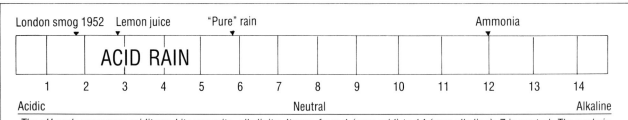

London smog 1952	Lemon juice	"Pure" rain							Ammonia			

ACID RAIN

| 1 | 2 | 3 | 4 | 5 | 6 | 7 | 8 | 9 | 10 | 11 | 12 | 13 | 14 |

Acidic   Neutral   Alkaline

The pH scale measures acidity and its opposite, alkalinity. It runs from 1 (very acid) to 14 (very alkaline); 7 is neutral. The scale is logarithmic so, for example, rain with pH of 4 is ten times as acid as rain with a pH of 5.

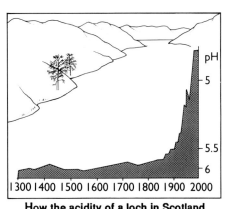

How the acidity of a loch in Scotland soared with industrialization.

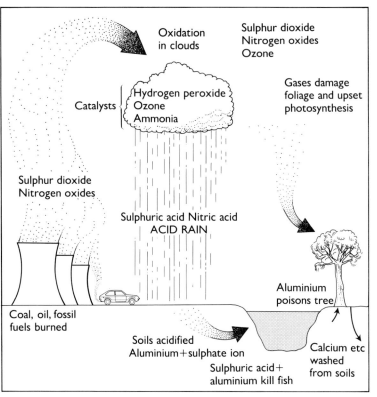

The chain from pollutants to acidified lakes, disappearing fish and dying trees

A History of Assault in Britain

Britain has an instructive history of assault by acid rain. Ever since the chimney became commonplace, ejecting fumes of burning fuel into the outside air, towns have suffered from air pollution. Smoke has been the most obvious problem. But sulphur, too, has had a part to play. Coal contains, typically, between 1 and 3 per cent sulphur which disappears up the chimneys as sulphur dioxide.

In December 1952, a pollution disaster hit London. A deadly 'smog' – a cold, black and sulphurous stew of air – hung over the city for almost a week, trapped by a blanket of warm air. It was the worst of a long series of 'peasouper' smogs that had hit London. It killed about 4000 people.

Smog irritated bronchial tubes, which became flooded with mucus. People choked to death or suffered heart attacks as they fought for breath.

At the time, doctors blamed the copious quantities of smoke and sulphur dioxide that accumulated in the smog. Scientists now believe that the formation of highly acid particles may have been important. One estimate puts the pH of London smog of 1952 at 1.6, rather more acid than lemon juice.

After 1952, a public outcry led to legislation banning the burning of smoky fuels in most towns and cities. This, coupled with the arrival of cheap North Sea gas, the growing use of electricity and a decision by the government to build the next generation of power stations outside urban areas, ensured that towns became vastly cleaner places.

But the government took no specific steps to limit emissions of sulphur dioxide from power stations burning coal and oil. Britain's output soared. By the mid-1970s, chimneys up to 300 metres high were putting more than 5 million tonnes of sulphur dioxide a year into the air over Europe. Other European countries emitted similar amounts. The result was that towns were cleaner, but sulphur dioxide spread in increasing amounts to the remotest corners of the continent. As later emerged, rainfall everywhere became more and more acid. □

The New Scientist

Stage 2 Obtain and then study some useful books on this subject. You may find your Geography department useful in addition to any libraries to which you have access.
For example:
Acid Rain by Fred Pearce (Penguin)
Ecology 2000 Edited by Sir Edmund Hillary (Michael Joseph)

Stage 3 Copy any useful diagrams you can find and assemble relevant photographs, if possible.

Stage 4 Use the headings below to help you to organize your article. You could alter them to suit your writing or make up your own.

In the soil – chemicals on the move

In the water – the poisoning of fish

In the forest – trees under attack

In the clouds – a cocktail of chemicals

In the future – prospects for a clean up

Stage 5 Produce a rough plan showing the order of your paragraphs.

Stage 6 Turn your plan into a first draft to discuss with your teacher and/or neighbour.

Stage 7 Produce your final assignment.

Special feature

The purpose of this assignment is to explore an individual response to the problems of the natural world. After reading part of Sir Edmund Hillary's introduction to his book *Ecology 2000*, you will be asked to develop your own understanding of this subject.

Ecology 2000

I have been lucky enough over the years to be involved in a number of adventures – in the Himalayas, the Antarctic and elsewhere. But slowly my values changed – success on an adventure was still important but I had an increasing interest in human relationships. I became involved in assistance programmes in Nepal – building schools and hospitals, bridges and water pipelines. Success on a mountain was no longer the only thing that mattered; to help others to improve their way of life became a prime target. And so it has gone on – still the odd adventure . . . jet boats up the Ganges; through Tibet to the east face of Everest; backpacking on Baffin Island in the Canadian Arctic . . . but more and more I've been getting involved with people and their problems – and very satisfying it has proved to be.

As my interest in people has grown so too has my awareness of our mutual environment and the importance of its conservation. After all, people and their environment are very closely related.

Thirty years ago conservation had not really been heard of. On our 1953 Everest expedition we just threw our empty tins and any trash into a heap on the rubble-covered ice at Base Camp. We cut huge quantities of the beautiful juniper shrub for our fires; and on the South Col at 26,000 feet we left a scattered pile of empty oxygen bottles, torn tents and the remnants of food containers.

The expeditions of today are not much better in this respect, with only a few exceptions. Mount Everest is littered with junk from the bottom to the top.

Since those years I have spent a great deal of time in the Himalayan Kingdom of Nepal. I have learned to understand the people, to enjoy their friendship and cheerfulness, and to gain an appreciation of some of their problems. One thing that has deeply concerned me has been the severe destruction that is taking place in their natural environment.

Population pressures are forcing the farmer higher and higher up the mountainside to find land where he can plant his crops. A large proportion of the forest cover has been destroyed in order to clear land for cultivation, to supply the local people with fuel and to produce firewood for trekking and climbing groups. The Nepalese are experts at ingenious and laborious terracing of their hillsides but when the monsoon rains come the surface soil is washed down into the streams, pours into the great Ganges river, flows out into the Bay of Bengal, and is finally deposited in the Indian Ocean. That valuable soil will never return.

The damage is not only being effected by the local people; foreign and international agencies are perhaps unwittingly causing their share as well. I have walked in from Kathmandu to the Mount Everest region perhaps thirty times and always enjoyed it, but a trip I made in March 1982 was different in many ways. We travelled by truck down the long valley to Dhologhat and crossed the big bridge built by Chinese engineers. Then it was a slow climb over the ridge and down to the road beside the Sun Kosi river. We bumped our way up the valley, crossing many washouts and giant slips where the steep slopes were subsiding into the river. Then we reached the depressing shanty town of Lamsangu.

Now for the first time I crossed the new Swiss bridge over the Sun Kosi river and climbed slowly to the east up the new Swiss road. It was a fantastic route – very steep and difficult. We climbed higher and higher up over a steep pass then down again for thousands of feet, winding around sharp corners and very rough sections above steep drops. After seven hours of spectacular driving we reached our destination at Kirantichap and here we pitched our tents.

I found Kirantichap completely changed. It used to be a tiny bazaar in a dip in the ridge with several huge pipal trees shading it. It had always been a pleasant place to camp, although it had brisk winds at times. The trees were still there and so was the wind but there were now many houses and a big bazaar. The construction work on the road had produced a dusty desert and strips of slums. The whole mountainside ahead of us up to Namdu and beyond – once so beautiful – was now terribly scarred from the work on the road. It was a depressing sight. The Swiss had gone to great trouble to build rock-retaining walls but on these steep loose hills the erosion would still be substantial. The engineering was superb but what possible use could the whole project have? Perhaps there were minor economic advantages for the area – no doubt food could be more easily transported out of Kathmandu – but what of the destruction of the mountainsides, the building of slums alongside the road, the devastating effect on the natural beauty of the area? Were the Swiss, I wondered, proud of what they were doing to this once stable and beautiful countryside?

Six days' walk further on we headed up the Solu valley taking the new high route above Beni. The whole beautiful Ringmo valley was scarred with a big new track, and the long hill down to Manedingma dropped steeply through wide stretches of destroyed forest. Why, I kept asking myself – the old road was nearly as short and very stable – why this obsession with destruction? There was only one reason. The United Nations were largely financing this work by donating imported grain and cooking oil. Without their support it would not have happened.

All the way up the Dudh Kosi river the track had been 'improved', with terrible scars and long stretches of eroded soil to show for it. Maybe the walking was a little easier and maybe the scars would heal again, but meanwhile vast quantities of soil would have washed out into the Indian Ocean and been lost for ever.

So I have become a keen and, I hope, a practical environmentalist. I am concerned not only about the deterioration of our environment in the affluent developed countries but in the poorer countries as well – those that simply do not have the finance to help themselves. I worry about the pollution in our great cities and in our many waterways. I even worry about the Antarctic and about the potential dangers facing that great remote continent.

Environmental problems are really social problems anyway. They begin with people as the cause, and end with people as victims. They are usually born of ignorance or apathy. It is people who create a bad environment – and a bad environment brings out the worst in people. Man and nature need each other, and by hurting one we wound the other. There is so much that needs to be done to halt the destruction of our world environment, so many prejudices and so much self-interest to be overcome. How can the situation possibly be changed in the time available?

My remaining hope is the amazing adaptability of human beings and the astonishing resilience of nature itself. Certainly the world and its human inhabitants are both changing, but we can hope that all the changes will not be bad. Perhaps humankind will start walking firmly in the direction of reconstruction and a better way of life. Maybe there is a good future for us all yet.

by *Edmund Hillary*

▼Assignment 20

Answer these questions as fully as you can.

1 In your own words, outline what you think to be the most important message contained in this extract.

2 What other 'junk' would you imagine a climber on Mount Everest might find today?

3 What examples of human mistreatment of the environment does Sir Edmund Hillary give here? Why do you think his attitude to conservation has changed?

4 In about 150–200 words describe an area near your home which you consider to have been spoiled by human beings. Include in your description reference to:
    a) what you think it might have looked like 30 years ago,
    b) what could be done to improve the area.
This could be a group report with individual contributions. Decide what age group you are writing for and what the 'message' of your description will be.

5 'Environmental problems are really social problems anyway.' What do you think is meant by this sentence? List any examples of behaviour that you can think of which demonstrate stupid or selfish use of the natural environment by people.

6 Imagine that you are given £5000 to spend on a project to:
    a) improve some part of your local environment,
    b) raise awareness of environmental issues in your area.

Describe how you would spend the money, who would be involved and what you would hope to achieve by such a project. You may wish to include diagrams, maps or photographs.

Key words

environmental chart
diagram evidence
statement scientific
conservation pollution
attitude

Key techniques

- using headings
- handling information as evidence
- using precise vocabulary that can be understood by a wider audience
- developing an argument
- understanding arguments
- predicting future events
- introducing a personal response to environmental writing

Writing about places requires particular skills of observation, imagination and understanding.

In the next six pages there are a number of different pieces of writing all stimulated by the same place – Cornwall.

The kingdom by the sea

A special train ticket I bought in Plymouth called 'The Cornish Explorer' allowed me to go anywhere in Cornwall, on any train. I travelled into the low shaggy hills, which were full of tumbling walls and rough stone houses, and yellow explosions of gorse bushes. I had lunch for eight pounds, which was twice as much as my ticket. The dining car was set for eighteen people, but I was the only diner. Elsewhere on the train, the English sat eating their sandwiches out of bags, munching apples and salting hard-boiled eggs. Times were hard. I realized that my lunch was overpriced, yet in a very short time there would be no more four-course lunch on these trains, no more rattling silverware, and no waiter ladling soup. But it was also ridiculous for me to be the only person eating: soup, salad, roast chicken and bread sauce, apple crumble, cheese and biscuits, coffee. There were two waiters in the dining car, and a cook and his assistant in the kitchen. The meal that most long-distance railway passengers had once taken for granted had now become a luxury, and Major Uprichard would soon be telling his grandchildren, 'I can remember when there were waiters on trains – yes, *waiters!*'

There were rolling hills until Redruth, and then the land was bleak and bumpy. There was only one working tin mine left in Cornwall (near St Just) but the landscape was scattered with abandoned mineworks, which looked like ruined churches in ghost villages. Cornwall was peculiarly uneven, with trees growing sideways out of stony ground, and many solitary cottages. On a wet day, its granite was lit by a granite-coloured sky and the red roads gleamed in a lurid way; it looked to be the most haunted place in England, and then its reputation for goblins seemed justified. It was also one of those English places which constantly reminded the alien, with visual shocks like vast battered cliffs and china clay waste dumps and the evidence of desertion and ruin, that he was far from home. It looked in many places as if the wind had screamed it of all its trees.

'I love the red earth,' Mrs Mumby said, staring out of the train window at the drizzle, and reminiscing. 'During the war I lived at Ross-on-Wye, in an antiquated old cottage. These Cornish cottages remind me of that. I don't like the architecture of today. Concrete jungle, I call it.'

Appearing to reply to this, Vivian Greenup said sharply, 'I've looked everywhere for my husband's walking-stick. My daughter brought it to the hospital, in case he might need it. After he died, I looked everywhere and couldn't find it.'

Mrs Mumby stared at Mrs Greenup and her expression seemed to say: *Why is Vivian running on like this about her dead husband's walking-stick?*

'It's quite a weapon,' Mrs Greenup said. 'You could use it as a weapon.'

We came to Penzance ('somewhat ambitiously styled the "Cornish Riviera"... John Davison, the Scottish poet, drowned himself here'). I changed trains and went back up the line about seven miles to St Erth, and there I waited in the rain for the next train to St Ives.

There were few pleasures in England that could beat the small three-coach branch-line train, like this one from St Erth to St Ives. And there was never any question that I was on a branch-line train, for it was only on these trains that the windows were brushed by the branches of the trees that grew close to the tracks. Branch-line trains usually went through the woods. It was possible to tell from the sounds at the windows – the branches pushed at the glass like mops and brooms – what kind of train it was. You knew a branch line with your eyes shut.

We went along the River Hayle and paused at the station called Lelant Saltings, which faced green-speckled mud flats. Hayle was across the water, with a mist lying over it. There were two more stops – it was a short line – and then the semi-circle of St Ives. It was Cornish, unadorned, a grey huddled storm-lit town on several hills and a headland, with a beach in its sheltered harbour. Today, in the rain, it was quiet, except for the five species of gulls that were as numerous now as when W. H. Hudson was here and wrote about them.

All the great coastal towns of England were a mixture of the sublime and the ridiculous. Here was the sublime climate and the pearly light favoured by watercolourists, the sublime bay of St Ives and the sublime lighthouse that inspired Virgina Woolf to write one of her greatest novels, and the sublime charm of the twisty streets and stone cottages. And there was the ridiculous; the postcards with kittens in the foreground of harbour scenes, the candy shops with authentic local fudge, the bumper stickers, the sweatshirts with slogans printed on them, the souvenir pens and bookmarks and dish towels, and the shops full of bogus handicrafts, carved crosses and pendants. These carvings at St Ives advertised 'Our Celtic Heritage – The Celts were famous for their courage and fighting qualities, which carried them before the birth of Christ from their homeland north of the Alps, across the known world...' Cornish pride was extraordinary, and it was more than pride. It had fuelled a nationalist movement, and though the last Cornish-speaking person died in 1777 (it was Dolly Pentreath of Mousehole), and Cornish culture today was little more than ghost stories and meat pies, there was a fairly vigorous campaign being fought for Cornwall to secede from England altogether. It was not for a vague alien like myself to say this was ridiculous, but it did seem to me very strange.

Across St Ives Bay were sandy cliffs and dunes, and I thought of walking along that shore to the village of Portreath – it was about twelve miles: I could do it before nightfall. But the rain was coming darkly down like a shower of smut, and I still had my Cornish Explorer ticket. So I walked to St Ives Head, where the Atlantic was riotous, then I returned to the station to wait for the little train to take me back to St Erth.

by *Paul Theroux*

The legend of Penrose

A section of this piece, indicated by . . . . . . has deliberately been left blank for you to complete.

'What remains of the old mansion of Penrose, in Sennen, stands on a low and lonely site at the head of a narrow valley through which a mill-brook winds, with many abrupt turns, for about three miles, thence to Penberth Cove.' These words, from the old book of *Hearthside Stories*, had imprinted themselves in my mind, for a modern map says nothing of lonely sites or winding brooks, and the red circle I had drawn about the name Penrose might cover, for all I knew, a caravan camp dumped above a stream.

Here is the trouble when searching for the past. Imagination conjures up bare hills and wilder shores, manors with tall chimneys flanked by courtyards, only to find, when catching up with the present, that rows of houses or perhaps a filling-station dominate the hill, that a smuggler's cove has beach-tents and the foundations of a Tudor home are hidden beneath a stuccoed Victorian villa or modern bungalow.

'We can only drive there and find out,' my son said firmly, 'and if there's nothing left . . .' He shrugged in resignation and we set forth once again, with maps and field-glass, to that 'promontory of slaughter', West Penwith. As we drove, some fifty miles or more, I told him the story in the same language as I remembered it, as it was no doubt told in countless cottages on winter nights before an open hearth in bygone days, with the rain beating upon the windowpanes outside.

'Long, long ago,' I said, 'some three hundred years or maybe more, there was an ancient family called Penrose, living in the manor house that bore their name, in Sennen parish. The country thereabouts was wild and naked, exposed to the salt wind from the sea, and in winter the rain fretted the wheat out of the ground, so that it was washed away and useless, the only land for cultivation being the close places between the hills. The head of the family in those days was Ralph Penrose, who as a young man had led a seafaring life, and when he succeeded to his father's estate so great still was his love for sailing and the sea that he built himself a ship and became what they called then a fair-trader, or, as we say today, a smuggler. He was never a pirate, as some of them were, or robbed the poor, but would sail across to France with his devoted crew, most of them poor relations who could find no better means of living, and then bring back merchandise to Sennen, and distribute it amongst the people in the neighbourhood and the members of his own household. He traded for the love of the game, as did his cousin William, as great an adventurer as himself.

'Sorrow came to Ralph one autumn, when his wife died of a fever, and from then onwards he seemed to take a dislike to the land, being at sea more than ever and taking his only son with him, a lad of seven. He would do this even in winter, leaving his estate to be managed by his younger brother John. One winter's night, before the turn of the year, Ralph Penrose was sailing home from France with his ship well laden, his crew in good heart and his cousin William and his young son aboard, when . . . . . .

. . . . . .

We came to Sennen village, and, filling up with petrol, asked for the farmhouse of Penrose. We were directed to take a road inland towards the valley, where a gate would set us on the track to the farm. The countryside, if no longer quite as wild and barren as the old book had described it, was nevertheless windswept, and as we approached the valley excitement grew. We found the gate and motored up the track, no building yet in sight. There was a bank to the right of us, and beyond, winding through sunken fields, ran the stream. As we turned a bend in the track and climbed the hill we saw farm-buildings, in the distance, outlined against the sky.

We had found Penrose.

by *Daphne Du Maurier*

▼**Assignment 21**   Answer these questions as fully as you can after reading both extracts.

1 Choose five words from each passage that sum up for you these two impressions of Cornwall.

2 'like ruined churches in ghost villages'

Choose three short extracts from the first passage, like the one above, which you think are particularly effective pieces of description. Explain why you chose each one.

3 Make a list of everything that you have learned about Paul Theroux by reading his impressions of Cornwall.

4 Reread the first two paragraphs of the second passage. In your own words describe the writer's feelings about going to places with a strong sense of the past.

5 'One winter's night, before the turn of the year, Ralph Penrose was sailing home from France . . .'

Continue this legend in your own way. Make it as atmospheric as you can. Include supernatural elements in your version.

6 Which of these two pieces of travel writing do you prefer and why? Use these questions to help you:

a) What might Ralph Penrose have been smuggling?
b) What would John Penrose have thought of his older brother?
c) Is the legend likely to end happily or not?
d) Why has the story of what happened to Ralph Penrose become a legend; what was so unusual about it?
e) What happened to the farm-buildings that Daphne du Maurier was travelling to see?

Descriptions

1 In groups read these descriptions. For each one agree:
  a) in your own words what it is saying,
  b) who you think it is written for,
  c) what you learn about the writer, (this will vary greatly)
  d) what you can say about the way it is written, its style.

NB Some of these were written by school students while staying in Zennor, Cornwall.

A The wild and remote coasts of Devon and Cornwall, the hidden caves and coves of Somerset and Dorset, and the rugged individualism of the inhabitants made the West Country famous for smuggling over a period of nearly a thousand years. Smuggling is mentioned in Magna Carta...

B In the parish of St Teath, a pack of hounds was once kept by an old squire named Cheney. How he or they died I can't learn; but on Cheney Downs the ghosts of the dogs are sometimes seen, and often heard, in rough weather.

C The road to Penzance is curvaceous and smooth. It almost tells you to drive slowly and take in the area. In Penzance there is the hustle and bustle of Cornish locals as they gather up their shopping. Knowing the Cornish to be very friendly and accepting I somehow feel very much an outsider. This is probably because of my overall tramp-like appearance!

D The ferns are dancing to the tune of the wind. Spiders wave on their silvery webs in the breeze. A stream trickles through the undergrowth towards the sea. In the distance a single trawler sits waiting for its haul.

E Perched on the hill above the wood stands Blisland village. It has not one ugly building in it, which is unusual in Cornwall, the houses are round a Green. Between the lichen-crested trunks of elm and ash that grow on the Green, you can see everywhere the beautiful moorland granite.

F I like Cornwall very much. It is not England. It is bare and dark and elemental, Tristan's land. I lie looking down at a cove where the waves come white under a low, black headland, which slopes up in bare green-brown, bare and sad under a level sky. It is old, Celtic, pre-Christian. Tristan and his boat, and his horn.

G Of all manner of vermin, Cornish houses are most pestered with rats, a brood very hurtful for devouring of meat, clothes and writings by day; and alike cumbersome through their crying and rattling, while they dance their gallop gallyards in the roof at night.

85

A short walk on the Hindu Kush

We set off at a quarter to eight. All three of us were now dressed alike in windproof suits, Italian boots and dark goggles. On our heads we wore our own personal headgear. It was essential to wear something as the heat of the sun was already terrific. Our faces were smeared with glacial cream and our lips with a strange-tasting pink unguent of Austrian manufacture. We looked like head-hunters.

At first the way led over solid rock which shone like lead, polished by the friction of thousands of tons of ice passing over it. It was only a surface colour; chipped, it showed lighter underneath, like the rest of the mountain, a sort of unstable granite. To the left was another lake, smaller than the lower one but more beautiful, the water bright blue, rippled by the wind, inviting us to abandon this folly. At last we reached the terminal *moraine*, the rock brought down by the glacier now locked across the foot of it in confusion. It was as if a band of giants had been playing cards with slabs of rock, leaving them heaped sixty feet high. Through this mess we picked our way like ants. From the depths of the *moraine* came the whirring of hidden streams. Above us the 'Son of Mir Samir' towered into the sky, and from its fastnesses came unidentifiable tumbling sounds.

At eight-thirty we reached the glacier, the first I had ever been on in my life. It was about a mile and a half long. The ice was covered at this, the shallow end, by about a foot of snow, frozen hard during the night but now melting rapidly. The water was spurting out of the foot of the glacier as if from a series of hosepipes.

We embarked on it, keeping close in under the snow slopes which rose sheer to the mountain on the right hand; now in the cold shadow of the 'son' we put on our crampons. Apart from the day in Milan when I had bought them in a hurry, it was the first time I had worn crampons. I didn't dare ask Hugh whether he had, but I noticed that his too were new.

'I do not wish to continue,' said Abdul Ghiyas, courageously voicing my own thoughts at this moment. It was obvious that he had never worn crampons from the difficulty he was having in adjusting them. 'My head is very bad.'

'My stomach is bad; the feet of Newby *Seb* are bad, yet we shall continue,' said Hugh.

Cruelly, we encouraged him to go on. Perhaps it was the effect of altitude that made us do so. At any rate we roped up and he allowed himself to be linked between us without demur.

We set off; Abdul Ghiyas with his awful head, Hugh with his stomach, myself with my feet and my stomach. Apart from these ills, we all agreed that we felt splendid, at least we could feel our legs moving.

'I think we've acclimatized splendidly,' said Hugh with satisfaction. I found it difficult to imagine the condition and state of mind of someone who had acclimatized badly ...

Somewhere above us was the summit but it was invisible, masked by the north-west buttress, smooth and unclimbable from the point where it was joined by the wall we were perched on. The wall itself was crowned with pinnacles of rock thirty feet high; at this moment we were in a dip between two of them.

Far away beyond the east glacier and a labyrinth of lesser mountains was a great mass of peaks, all snow-covered; one of them like an upturned cornet.

'That's Point 5953, the one we're going to climb if we have time after this one,' Hugh said.

The whole thing was on such a vast scale; I felt a pigmy, powerless . . .

By now all three of us were tired. The journey over the glacier was a test of endurance. Our goggles were steamed up; we moved infinitely slowly. As we neared the end of the glacier, my horizon dropped more and more until it took in nothing but the loop of rope between myself and Abdul Ghiyas and the ice immediately underfoot. In the ice were mysterious holes eight inches deep and perhaps an inch wide. It was as though they had been made with a drill or else as though a plug had been removed. At the bottom there was sometimes a little earth or a single stone. The glacier was now in full melt: from beneath it came the whirring of invisible streams and when we reached the foot the water roared from it like a mill race in flood . . .

I had never seen such a mountain. It was nothing like anything we had seen in Wales. To someone like myself, completely unversed in geological expressions, it seemed to be made from a sort of shattered granite; 'demoralized' was the word that rose

continually to my lips while, as the thaw continued and progressively larger rocks bounded past us on their way to the glacier, the childish 'it isn't fair' was only repressed with difficulty.

To cheer one another in this hour, when the first intimations of fatigue were creeping up on us and while whoever was leader was scrabbling awfully with his feet for a possible foot-hold where none existed, we pretended to be Damon Runyon characters trying to climb a mountain. Hugh was Harry the Horse.

'Dose Afghans soitinly build lousy mountains' was what he said, as a particularly large boulder went bouncing past us over the edge and on to the glacier below with a satisfying crash.

At eleven we reached the foot of a gully and, with the help of the pamphlet, which we consulted unashamedly in moments of crisis, ascended it.

By this time, by the application of common sense and without the help of the book, we had evolved a far swifter method of roped climbing than we had ever practised before . . .

Like Red Indians made cunning by suffering, we were learning by experience. That what we were doing is common mountaineering practice is a measure of our ignorance.

In this way we ascended this nasty gully, the head of which was jammed with loose rocks, all ready to fall, and at eleven-thirty came out on to snow on top of the east ridge.

It was a tremendous moment. We had reached it too low down and further progress towards the top was made impossible by a monster pinnacle of extreme instability. Nevertheless, the summit looked deceptively close. The altimeter after a good deal of cuffing read 18,000 feet.

'That's about right,' Hugh said. 'Splendid, isn't it!'

'I'm glad I came.'

'Are you really?' he said. He sounded delighted.

'I wouldn't have missed it for anything.' And I really meant it.

Two thousand feet below us, like an enormous new frying-pan sizzling in the sun, was the east glacier. Away to the east the view was blocked by a bend in the ridge in which we sat, but to the south the mountains seemed to surge on for ever ...

by *Eric Newby*

1 At first the way led over solid rock which shone like lead ...

This is the first of a number of comparisons made by the writer in an attempt to bring the description of this difficult walk alive. Make a list of three others used in this passage. For each one describe the effect that the image creates for you when reading it.

2 Imagine you were Eric Newby. Make a list of the different emotions you were experiencing throughout the walk. Record these in note form.

7.45 Very excited. Also feeling nervous and slightly ridiculous.

8.30 At the glacier- amazed by its size, suddenly very scared.

3 What do you learn about the writer from this passage?

Journeys

Give a brief talk about a journey that you have undertaken which was in some way significant for you.

It might be:
● a walk with friends, family, girl/boyfriend
● a climb or expedition undertaken with your school or with some other organization
● an exploration of a new place while on holiday at home or abroad
● a time when you were lost or in danger

Try and communicate something about the place *and* your reactions to it.

◣Assignment 22

In this assignment you are going to write about an area of the world of your own choosing. Because this can only be achieved through direct observation on your part, several different methods are suggested here. The final choice must be your own.

Whichever method you choose try to:
- use your own style,
- show some understanding of your chosen area,
- allow your own personality to be evident by the way you respond to your travelling, for example, your feelings towards certain types of place.

ROUTE 1

Holiday writing

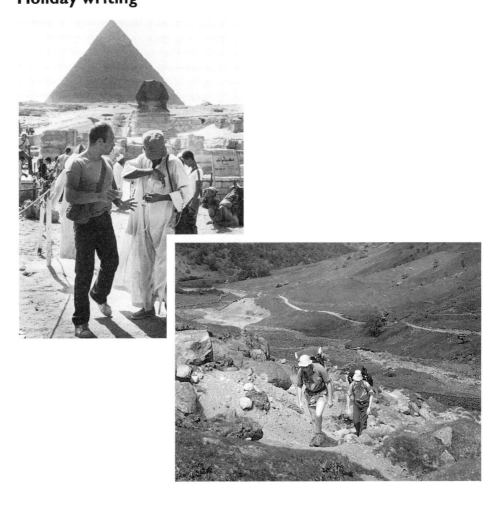

Stage 1 ▼ Gather information about an area you have visited on holiday: photographs, tourist information, brochures, etc.

Stage 2 ▼ Talk to people who live and work there.

Stage 3 ▼ Plan and structure a piece of writing choosing the parts of your holiday experience that are most appropriate.

Remember that this is not meant to be a holiday diary or a tourist guide, but something which shows your responses to a new place, to those who live there, and how this has affected you.

ROUTE 2

Magical mystery tour

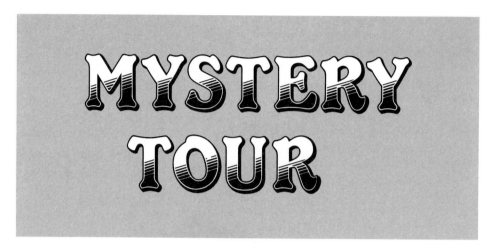

Stage 1   With a friend, take a bus or train to an area near your home that you do not know.

Stage 2   Write an article with a particular set of readers in mind, for example, for a local newspaper or local magazine.

Stage 3   Give your article a strong focus, for example, on traditional crafts, the natural world, local people, young people in the area, shopping facilities, sporting opportunities.

ROUTE 3

Home sweet home

...INTERVIEW RESIDENTS OF THE AREA WHO HAVE LIVED THERE SOME WHILE ....

Write about somewhere you know well for inclusion in a school magazine.

Stage 1   Research its history, its legends, its current image.

Stage 2   Interview residents of the area who have lived there for some while.

Stage 3   By including details that *only* someone who knows the area as you do could cover, create the necessary interest in your article.

ROUTE 4

Danger and excitement

Describe an area of the country that you have found challenging. For example, the Scottish Highlands during a storm, an expedition to Wales, an unfamiliar city or any other suitable place. Include your emotional responses to your chosen landscape and your own experience of it.

Key words

impression landscape people journey legend character

Key techniques

- developing skills of observation
- using comparisons to bring out your own responses to places (eg 'like ruined churches in ghost villages')
- conveying strong responses to a place and its mood
- developing an individual style
- researching a particular area of a country
- conveying 'the past' of a place
- using the idea of a journey
- focusing on people

Talking as writing

Interviews and conversations can be transferred to the page to produce a less formal style of writing.

Read this account of Philip Rigden's job as a dustman. It was based on an interview with Danny Danziger.

All in a day's work

I enjoy it, but like any other job it gets a bit of a routine after a bit, you know. But I get up in the morning and pull myself up and say, 'OK, you know it's a good job this really.' I mean it's handy for me, it's only five minutes down the road, and I get up on the hills and it's gorgeous, especially in the summer.

The area around here is lovely. It's turning into a town now, but it used to be a tiny village, the sort of place you stopped on your way to somewhere else, a journey's resting place. It's just a nice little town with a few of the old Yorkshire cotton mills.

A lot of people have said, 'You don't look like a dustman,' so I usually say, 'What does a dustman look like?' When I go out I dress in right with-it stuff, I suppose that's it, I've always been very smart in my appearance. I get a perverted sort of pleasure out of saying I'm a dustman. I'm proud to be a dustman, any road.

I don't put a lot of mental activity into it. I work hard physically, but I wouldn't like to say, 'I'm Philip Rigden the great dustman.' I try and be a good dustman, I'm conscientious, but it doesn't take a lot up here to be a good dustman. It's not the most important thing to me. A job is a job. I need to pay the mortgage and pay my other bills. I wouldn't say I sweep roads therefore I must be this sort of person, I'd say I sweep roads to earn a living to make some money so I can pay bills, full stop.

It's all go, from as soon as you get there. You get the wagon ready, go pick the lads up, and you're out, and there's not a minute to spare. Sometimes to keep up to your bonus, you're running, there just isn't enough time. You've got to empty so many bins in your allotted time for the week, you get so many hours for each round and you're timed for one minute, forty-five seconds for each bin, and you have to keep up to that all the time. Management says if you get your full bonus, you should be absolutely shattered at the end of the week. To achieve top bonus regular is very hard work. The average dustman walks twenty-two miles a day. I'm not kidding. The time-and-motion man came round with our gang a couple of weeks back and he clocked twenty-two miles on his chart, and that's as well as humping bins.

Because you're walking so much and carrying so much, your legs and your hips feel the strain. A few weeks back I hadn't done any dustbins, I'd just been driving for about a month, and when they put me on bins again, I had to go and sit in the cab for about an hour, I felt dizzy and I was out of breath. They took me home, actually, I was that bad.

A lot of people who I talk to, they say, 'Well, dustbin men never speak to you nowadays, they're right surly, they just come and empty your bin and they're off,' but it's because we're so busy.

I'm on the perimeter round at the moment, and there's three of us. We do all the farms way out, little hamlets, Hade Edge, Farnley Tyas, there's Tinker's Monument – that's not official that, everyone knows it as Tinker's Monument – Victoria, Hepworth, there's loads of little places. I'm driver loader which means if there's a driver or loader off, I'll take their place, so I move around from gang to gang. I like moving around although it's not always top money because you usually go where there's trouble, where they're lagging behind or something like that.

Today it was me and Barry and Frank. Frank's a mate of mine and Barry's a bit of a character, he's well known in this area, Barry Lee, ask anybody and they'll know Barry. So I've been talking to him, but we're behind on this round and I got stuck in the snow and we didn't get finished on time, so we're still behind for tomorrow. What else happened today . . . the dog tried to bite me, that's a constant problem, the women'll come out and say, 'It's all right, he won't bite you,' and you're trying to shake him off your leg.

I try and enjoy myself while I'm at work, you have to make the most of it. So I look around at all the beautiful things that are going on around me, and I like talking to people. I think about how long it's going to take us to do such a street and how long it's going to take me to get down to the bottom and all this, and then I think about my life, and I have a couple of mates, and we talk, we swap yarns about women and booze, you know.

They're fine lads. There are some characters. We're shouting and bawling at each other during the day because the pressure's on to get the work done, so we get a bit ratty sometimes, but then when the work's over we'll have a pint together, so it's nothing serious. It's the hardest job physically I've ever done. It keeps you fit, but if you're getting on a bit it doesn't do you any good.

If people all worked together I think it would be a lot nicer. They could help by putting the dustbin neat instead of overflowing it, and making it easier access. I had a syringe in my leg today! I picked a bag up and it swung, and this hypodermic syringe was sticking through, and I don't know what they used it for, it could be anything, could be AIDS, stuck right in, I'll have to put it in the Accident Book. I forgot all about it. But I'd say most people are considerate. If there's broken glass in the rubbish, they'll wait for you and say, 'There's some glass in there but I wrapped it up in paper,' and you say, 'Fair enough.' Most people give you a tip at Christmas time. You can make a nice bonus out of that. I'd say on the whole people do consider the dustbin men, it's just that when you're rushing about you don't want to get one that's overflowing.

I'll get shot for saying this, but there is one big perk. It's called tatting, it's like junk, what people throw out; all sorts of stuff, televisions, crockery, I got that clock there, that pewter mug, the coal-scuttle, anything, books – I've got quite a lot of interesting books out of that. You get to know when you pick a bag up, you can feel if it's rubbish, or if there might be something in it. It does slow you down a little.

I go to night school. I'm studying art. Just passed my O-levels; I'm studying A-levels now. I really like Leonardo da Vinci. I think he had a brilliant mind, a beautiful mind, he was so intelligent. Not just an artist, inventor as well. He had style, didn't he?

I do a lot of portraits of the boys, and I do a lot of buildings, old buildings. Well, my line of work is excellent for having a look and seeing what'll make a good picture while I'm out on the job. The lads will say, 'There you are, Phil, there's a good one there.' It's great. And on the weekends or at night I'll go sketching. I look around the beautiful valley with the sun setting and that inspires me, and first thing in the morning, if we get up and stop for breakfast and it's a nice clear, crisp morning, and the sun's just coming out, that inspires me, plus we always see lots of squirrels, rabbits, foxes, hares, sheep, you know, things like that inspire me.

The lads do tend to tease me. They'll say, 'Hello, Picasso,' or they call me a piss artist. I get my leg pulled all the time – 'Do a drawing of this', and it's an old dustbin or something like that. They're always taking the Mickey. But they are interested, they ask me a lot of questions, and if I get them on my own, we'll have a serious conversation about art.

I'd rather paint. I'd rather be an artist full time, it's what I want to do, I'd be more content if I was an artist. I

could put in eight hours a day quite easily instead of putting in eight hours a day emptying dustbins.

I'm frustrated I haven't got the time to study. I mean an ordinary artist, he gets more practice in one day than I get in a couple of weeks. I know I could do better in my art if I had more time to study, but because I work hard physically, I get home, I don't feel like doing it sort of thing, so I do get frustrated.

I've done a lot of pen-and-ink sketching. I've done so many of them and sold so many, it's boring me now. So I'm starting on to colours, coloured pencils, oil paints, what I can afford. Coloured pencils are the cheapest so I'm into that now. I'm trying to improve my application of colour.

I can see myself being a fairly good artist after about another five years. Whether I'll make a living at it, I don't think I will, I think I'll remain a dustman. Or maybe try and work my way up in the dustbins, supervisor or something like that, but that takes a lot of concentration so I wouldn't be able to concentrate on my art then. I'm being realistic. I know what I want to be in the next five years, I want to be a full-time artist – but being realistic, I think I'll spend the next five years on the bins.

Maybe I am more optimistic than I'm letting on, it's funny, you don't want to reveal all your dreams to a stranger. You know, you dream about being famous – it just seems absolutely ridiculous, but it's not actually fame that I want to achieve, I want to give people a message. I can't communicate in words, as you can see, but I can do it through art. Peace, love, beauty, truth, that's what it's all about.

by Philip Rigden

1 Imagine you were the interviewer for this piece. In groups, make up a list of the questions you would have prepared to produce the information given by Philip Rigden.

For example:

> a) Do you enjoy your work?
> b) Would you describe your job as hard work?

2 Make a list of any questions that you might have added *during* the interview because of the answers Philip Rigden was giving you. Look particularly carefully at the second part of the extract.

3 In your group discuss:
   a) what you have found out about Philip's attitudes to life,
   b) what you found most interesting or unusual about this piece.

Assignment 23

Stage 1   Prepare a list of ten questions to ask somebody about his/her job. You could choose someone at school, for example, your headteacher, a caretaker, a cleaner, a secretary or someone you know with a very different type of job.

Stage 2   Tape your interview, remembering to add other questions depending on the information you receive from your 'subject'.

Stage 3   Write up your interview under the title *All in a day's work*. Use the same first-person style adopted by Danny Danziger in the piece you have just read, without including any of your questions.

A style of writing very close to speech can be a particularly effective way of exploring more emotional topics.

Rosemary left school at sixteen instead of taking her A levels to marry the father of her baby. Eleven years later, read what she has to say as she reflects on her life.

Falling for love

When I look back it is hard to remember exactly how I felt when I thought I was pregnant. I know I was scared, but that was knowing I had to tell my parents. I felt I'd let them down, and that is something I still feel guilty about even now. It was much easier for my husband to tell his parents, and they took it much more easily than mine did. Now I can see why that was but at the time I couldn't really understand. Within my husband's family, to marry and have your children young is quite a normal thing to do. Both his mother and grandmother were married at sixteen, although his mum was twenty before she had her first child. They also didn't have particularly high expectations for my husband careerwise. He had a relatively secure job, the money wasn't too bad and the fact that he was going to marry and have a child wasn't going to change that. They were shocked, of course, when he first told them, but they were definitely able to accept it more easily than my parents did.

My mum and dad probably had high expectations of me, something I can only really understand now that I have children of my own. They probably had their own plans for me to take my A-levels, go to university or college, then a good job before settling down to marriage and babies. It really must have been a great disappointment to them. It is still quite hard for me to talk or write about this. I feel really guilty that I let them down. My dad died nearly two years ago and I know he was proud of his three grandsons but I would have liked him to see that I was attempting to do something with my

life now. I think it took a long time for him to come to terms with the fact that I was having a baby and getting married. He wasn't the kind of man who really showed his true feelings and I realize that it must have been a very difficult time for him, as it was for me. It is said that men are very protective towards their daughters and I'm sure this was definitely the case with us.

I remember breaking down and telling my mum I thought I was pregnant, but I think she'd already guessed. I couldn't tell my dad, she had to do that for me. Telling my boyfriend was much easier, he was shocked of course, but pleased as well, and very keen to get married as soon as possible. His parents were all for this, and very keen to help us and support us. My parents were rather harder to persuade. First of all they tried to persuade me to have an abortion but that was a non-starter. I knew that I was going to have my baby and keep it. Then they said that I could have the baby and stay at home with their support but not get married until I was sure that was what I wanted. However, at the time I was determined that I was going to get married before the baby was born. His parents backed us up, offering us a home until we could get one of our own.

I left school at Christmas and married in the March. It was quite a nice wedding, in a registry office, with a meal afterwards for close family, and a party at my husband's home in the evening for our friends. Looking back now I wish I'd had something a bit more memorable, but at the time I just wanted something quiet. I can't

say I really enjoyed it very much.

We settled down to married life, living with my in-laws which was never easy with so many in the household. The pregnancy went well, I was reasonably healthy, but always seemed rather embarrassed by my condition. My son was born in the July, and then our problems really started. For the first six months he was a very difficult, demanding baby, always hungry, sleeping very little and far too much for a young couple like us to cope with alone. I can honestly say that if it hadn't been for

my mother-in-law I don't think we would have been able to. She used to take him into their room sometimes at night so we could get some sleep. We were always able to get out together on our own for a night out because there was always a babysitter at home.

Whey my son was six months old we got a council house and it was really nice to be on our own as a family. Money was quite tight but we managed all right. I went to evening classes to do shorthand and typing so I could get a job to help out. Then

120 things began to look up. We got a council house exchange to the area that my husband came from, opposite his parents, in fact. We still live in this house, but we have bought it now and renovated it all. Then my husband got a better-paid job.

Because of this, I didn't have to go out to work. We had our second child Nicholas who is now seven, and David 130 who is three. Both were planned. I always said I'd had one child who wasn't planned and that was enough. I wanted my children reasonably spaced apart so I didn't have to cope with more than one baby at a time. It certainly was lovely being able to announce to people I was pregnant without feeling any shame or embarrassment. These two were 140 definitely easier babies to look after and I often wonder if it was because I was happier and more relaxed during the pregnancies and whether it was because I was older and better able to cope with them.

Since David arrived I felt it was time to return to studying, so I started to go to night-school. The first year I began with O-level sociology which I really enjoyed. Realizing I could do 150 other things as well as be a wife and mother gave me the confidence to get a job as a market research interviewer, which I have been doing for the past eighteen months. Last year I took the A-level sociology course and this year I am taking A-level psychology. I don't know what I'm going to do with these exams but at the moment I enjoy the challenge of 160 doing the courses and taking the exams. At least my brain is still working after all those years at home. I am happier now than I have been for the last eleven years. I have my husband and children. I have my job and a little independence and I am continuing my education.

When I look back at myself as I was then, I think how naive I was and 170 how immature. I thought I knew it all when in fact I knew nothing. Everything my husband and I have now we have had to struggle for. We have done everything the wrong way round and for us it has worked out fine, but it hasn't been plain sailing.

▼ Assignment 24

These questions are designed to help you explore your understanding of Rosemary's not uncommon situation.

1 The two sets of parents reacted very differently to the news of Rosemary's pregnancy. (lines 1–29) In your own words describe these two reactions.

2 'It is said that men are very protective towards their daughters.' (lines 53–4) Is this true? Describe your own parents' protectiveness towards you.

3 In what ways do you think parents' attitudes are different towards daughters and sons? To help you explore this idea, you could include in your answer any relevant incidents from your own experience or those of your friends.

4 'I remember breaking down and telling mum I thought I was pregnant.' (lines 56/8) How do you think Rosemary told her mother? Write out Rosemary's diary account of this difficult day as you think she might have written it.

5 Make a list of some of the problems you think Rosemary might have experienced as a very young mother in her first year of marriage.

6 'Realizing I could do other things . . . months.' (lines 150/5) Write out another diary extract covering a day of Rosemary's life as an interviewer. Try and suggest the ways in which her life is very different to what it was eleven years ago.

7 For Rosemary things 'worked out fine'. Describe the options that you would be considering if you had been in *either* Rosemary's *or* her husband's situation.

In the law court the relationship between talking and writing is of great importance. Accurate reports of what was said during criminal activity can become particularly significant.

Read this speech given by Christmas Humphreys, the prosecuting counsel, during the trial of Christopher Craig and Derek Bentley on December 1952. Both men had pleaded not guilty to the charge of murder.

'Before the police arrived, Craig and Bentley had climbed the gate to the premises and were already on the roof which stood twenty-two feet high. It was flat and had four roof lights, the head of a lift shaft and an emergency door opening on to it.

The police-car was quickly on the spot. Out of it ran Police Constables Fairfax, Harrison, and McDonald. They were soon over the gate and looking around for access to the roof.

There was a moon, but it was hidden behind cloud most of the time. The police, therefore, used flash-lamps. A beam of light far below warned Craig of what was happening. He is reported to have said, 'Coppers!' and led Bentley into hiding behind the lift shaft.

Fairfax, leader of the police and the most agile physically, climbed up a drain-pipe and got on to the roof. He saw Craig and Bentley and walked towards them.

'I am a police-officer,' he said. 'Come out from behind the stack.'

Craig answered:

'If you want us, ... well come and get us!'

'All right,' said Fairfax, leaping forward.

He grabbed Bentley by the arm. With Bentley in custody he turned and pursued Craig round the stack; but Bentley got away and shouted an observation, heard by three separate officers in the darkness by three separate places, which may be, in your view, the most important that Bentley made that night.

'Let him have it Chris . . .'

The most immediate reply to that comment by Bentley was a loud report, and Fairfax was hit on the shoulder with what turned out to be a bullet from the gun which Craig held. That observation was not only heard by Constable Fairfax grappling with two men in the dark on the roof, but by another officer, McDonald, who was at that moment climbing up the same drain-pipe, and by another officer who had arrived from an entirely different direction, P.C. Harrison.

All three heard it, and all three heard the shot which followed immediately upon it. That statement was a deliberate incitement to Craig to murder Constable Fairfax. It was spoken to a man whom he, Bentley, clearly knew had a gun. That shot began a fight in the course of which P.C. Miles was killed; that incitement covered the whole of the shooting thereafter; even though at the time of the actual shot which killed P.C. Miles, Bentley was in custody and under arrest.

P.C. Fairfax was not seriously wounded. The bullet glanced across his shoulder and only cut the skin.

Then Craig fired again. P.C. Fairfax dragged Bentley and worked him round to the doorway, where both of them could get cover from the shooting which was still coming from the direction of the lift. Bentley said to Fairfax, 'He'll shoot you.'

Nevertheless, they reached the staircase head in safety, and both took cover behind it. So Fairfax has been alone upon the roof with two men, one of whom he now holds and the other is shooting at them; but just about that moment P.C. McDonald arrives up the drainpipe. Apparently he is a big and heavy man, and had difficulty in getting up the last few feet, and Fairfax went and helped him up.

Fairfax said to McDonald, 'He got me in the shoulder.' Bentley, who you will remember, is under arrest with Fairfax at the time, said, 'I told the silly . . . . not to use it.' That means, you may think, that Bentley knew quite well that Craig had a gun, and that he knew that Craig at least meant to use it. But that statement, of course, is completely contradicted by Bentley's earlier statement, heard by three police-officers. 'Let him have it, Chris.'

Fairfax, now with the reinforcement of McDonald, shouted to Craig, 'Drop your gun.' Craig's reply was, 'Come and get it.' and another shot was fired. It seems to have missed everything; but that shot was probably at P.C. Harrison who had climbed from the ground up to the roof of No. 25 and from where he got on to the sloping roof of Barlow and Parker's warehouse. P.C. Harrison, although he heard these shots being fired, crept along the gutter towards Craig. To do so he was lying on his back with his feet in the gutter, and was completely helpless.

Presenting a sitting target, he could do nothing whatsoever to avoid such shots as were fired towards him as he lay or crawled or crept along. Craig saw him and deliberately fired at him, certainly once, probably twice. Harrison, realizing that it was suicide to attempt to go further, crawled back, got down, raced round to the door of the main building and with the other officers, shortly came up that staircase, (the one leading to the roof) when a key had been obtained, and joined in the fight on the roof.

Meanwhile, to come back to what was happening on the roof, McDonald asked Fairfax, after these shots had been fired at Harrison, 'What sort of gun has he got?' Bentley still under arrest, cut in and said, 'He's got a .45 Colt and plenty of ammunition for it too.'

Down below, the police, as I have stated, had found somebody with the keys, had got the door open at the foot and came racing up the stairs. They were led by P.C. Miles. Miles, when he got to the head of the staircase, went straight out on to the roof. Craig fired again. Miles fell dead with a bullet straight between the eyes. Craig then came from behind the stack holding the gun in both hands and fired again at the stairs.

P.C. Harrison was next out of the doorway. Stepping over Miles' body, he threw at Craig all he had to throw, his truncheon, a bottle he had picked up somewhere and a block of wood. The reply by Craig was quite clear: 'I am Craig. You have just given my brother twelve years. Come on, you coppers. I'm only sixteen.'

And another shot was fired.

Then Bentley, at that moment technically under arrest and with men who were being shot at, said, 'You want to look out; he'll blow your heads off.'

At that moment they began to take him downstairs, and he shouted, 'Look out, Chris; they're taking me down.'

The reply from Craig was another burst of firing.

You gentlemen of the jury, will have to interpret all the evidence in this case, and you will have to interpret that further observations by Bentley, made, although he is technically under arrest, while he is still on the roof where the fight is going on and, to all intent and purposes, in the presence of Craig. He is being taken down by the police-officers and he calls out, 'Look out, Chris; they're taking me down.' Was that a further invitation? Cry for help? What was it? The result was clear: a further burst of firing by Craig.

Then P.C. Jaggs arrived. He came up the drain-pipe and came round at the head of the stairs. Fairfax had gone down with Bentley, and at the foot of the stairs he was given a gun. That shows how long this fight had been going on, for the police, hearing the firing, had had time to send to the police station and get firearms from the proper authorized supply, and return.

Fairfax was given a gun with which to return to the fight. As he got to the top of the stairs, now for the first time armed, he shouted out to Craig, 'Drop your gun, I also have a gun,' and he ran straight at him in the darkness in a semi-circle, firing
210 twice. He missed. Down below in the garden was P.C. Lowe, because the police reinforcements were such that the whole building was now surrounded, and he from his position in the garden looked up and saw Craig outlined against the sky on a railing which is close to the top of the lift shaft or stack.

Craig above at the railing was
220 heard by several officers to make a little speech; various officers heard part of it, but Lowe seems to have heard most of it completely. The answer to Fairfax coming out with a gun and shouting to Craig, 'Drop your gun, I also have a gun,' was this: 'Yes, it's a Colt .45. Are you hiding behind a shield, is it bullet-proof? Are we going to have a shooting match? It's
230 just what I like. Have they hurt you Derek?' Now that is Derek Bentley, who at that moment was being taken down the stairs by police-officers after he had called out, 'Look out, Chris; they're taking me down.'

Officers then heard four clicks, clicks as of a gun the trigger of which had been pulled but for some reason has not fired and then a shot, and
240 then a cry from Craig, 'There, it's empty.' and then he dived from the roof into the darkness down below, which is 20 to 25 feet. He seems to have fallen beyond the glass of the greenhouse, that is to say he jumped just short of the greenhouse. As he jumps he throws his revolver; the revolver goes through the glass and makes that hole in the roof, and is later found in the greenhouse. 250

He falls short and in some way breaks his wrist, hurts his back and the middle of his chest or breastbone, and there lies injured. As he jumps he calls out, 'Give my love to . . .' It sounds like a girl's name. I do not know what; but when he arrived below, a police-officer, not knowing, of course, whether he was still armed or not, or how injured he was or was not, 260 jumped at him, and as he holds him down, Craig says, 'I wish I was . . . dead. I hope I've killed the lot.' You will bear that in mind if any question arises as to the intent with which he was shooting at police-officers on this night.

On him was found a different kind of sheath-knife. So he had a knife as well as a gun, and Bentley had a knife 270 as well as a knuckle-duster. The gun fight, such as it was, was at an end. Constable Fairfax was taken to hospital, so was Craig, and P.C. Miles to the mortuary.

The case for the prosecution is this: that Craig deliberately and wilfully murdered that Police Constable, P.C. Miles, and thereafter glorified in the murder; that Bentley 280 incited Craig to begin the shooting and although technically under arrest at the actual time of the killing of Miles, was party to that murder and equally responsible in law.'

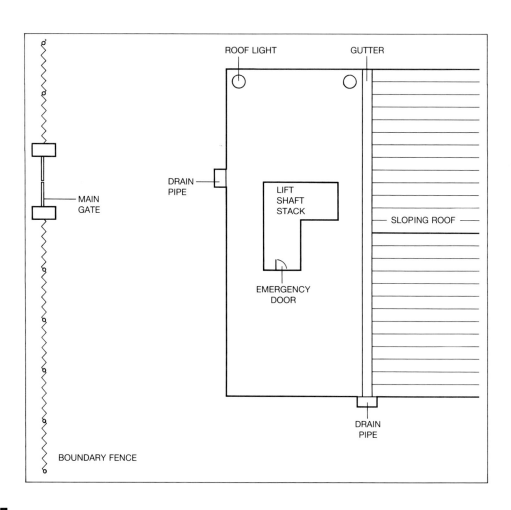

ROOF LIGHT   **GUTTER**

DRAIN PIPE

MAIN GATE

LIFT SHAFT STACK

SLOPING ROOF

EMERGENCY DOOR

DRAIN PIPE

BOUNDARY FENCE

▼ Assignment 25

This assignment asks you to imagine you are involved in the Craig and Bentley Trial from three different points of view.

1 Using the diagram above, write the detailed report of the incident that P.C. Fairfax produced for the trial, after he had been discharged from the hospital. Start your report from the time P.C. Fairfax arrived on the roof up to the moment when he was given a gun with which to return to the fight. The report begins . . .

'I climbed up a drain-pipe and got onto the roof. On seeing Craig and Bentley I walked towards them and said, 'I am a police-officer. Come out from behind the stack . . .'

2 In his case for the prosecution, Christmas Humphreys asks the jury to:

'. . . interpret all the evidence in this case.'

On two occasions during the scene on the roof Derek Bentley is quoted:

'Let him have it Chris.' (line 42)
'Look out Chris; they're taking me down.' (lines 172–3)

You are a member of the jury that sat at the trial of Craig and Bentley in December, 1952. How would you argue against the following jury member who seems to be speaking for the majority of the jury:

a) 'I think that when Bentley shouted "Let him have it, Chris." he was inviting Craig to shoot P.C. Fairfax – in other words "Shoot him, Chris."'

b) 'Obviously, when Bentley shouted out, "Look out Chris; they're taking me down." he was warning Craig about the activities of the police and, I think, preparing him for what was to follow – an armed attack on Craig by the police.'

3 In his defence Derek Bentley's father argues that Christmas Humphreys' interpretation of the facts of what actually happened on the roof is incorrect. He makes the following points about Humphreys' case for the prosecution:

a) 'It's strange because our Derek never ever called Craig "Chris", but always "Kid" or "Kiddo" and yet the police said they heard Derek say "Let him have it, Chris." I can't understand it.'

b) 'In Christmas Humphreys' case for the prosecution he says that our Derek "got away" (lines 36–42). As I understand it though, our Derek never left P.C. Fairfax's side, after his arrest, throughout the whole of the incident.'

c) 'Our Derek never attempted to attack or even escape from P.C. Fairfax, who was injured, yet he had the opportunity to.'

d) 'When P.C. Miles was shot dead our Derek was nowhere near Craig. In fact he was actually in custody with P.C. Fairfax. What I want to know is how can our Derek be accused of a crime that was committed when he was already under arrest?'

e) 'They found a knuckle-duster and a knife on our Derek when they brought him down off that roof. Now if my son was on Craig's side why didn't he use them against P.C. Fairfax or any other police-officer? That's what I want to know.'

f) 'My son Derek actually attempted to help the police on that roof and on several occasions offered information to them. So how could he be seen to be against the police and attempting to help Craig?'

In the light of the above points, and by checking them against Christmas Humphreys' case for the prosecution, imagine you are Bentley's father and write a letter of appeal to the Home Secretary.

The letter could begin like this:

> Dear Sir,
>   I appeal to everyone in this country to give careful consideration to the following vital facts in the case of the State versus my son, Derek Bentley...

Key words
interview conversation
informal experience
question attitude

Key techniques
- planning suitable interview questions
- interviewing sensitively
- using interviews to produce writing
- interpreting oral evidence
- selecting oral material
- writing in a conversational style

UNIT 9 *letters and diaries*

For many hundreds of years a diary has been one way of recording detailed observations of personal feelings, historical or political events and the changing natural world.

Nature diaries

Read these two collections of diary extracts about the natural world in Spring.

March 12th

Although the weathermen predicted snow and sleet in March, I cannot remember one rainy day in the last two weeks. The sounds of lawn-mowers, tractors and birds herald the spring.

Last Tuesday I saw the most extraordinary thing. I was trying hard to talk to a very polite and kindly couple about a print that they wished to purchase, but my eyes were continually drawn to the window. In the end, ignoring the poor man's questions completely, I drew his attention to the extraordinary fierce battle taking place just beyond the window ledge. One large, glossy, female blackbird stood, head cocked to one side, watching two somewhat bedraggled female blackbirds fight until I was frightened that one of them might be seriously injured. The two birds went over and over, wings flapping on the grassy slope. Eventually one bird was actually standing on the breast of the other. The noise and wing flapping went on for a while, then stopped. Both birds faced one another, a distance of about four inches between them. Then they lowered themselves slowly on to their stomachs, opening their wings and flattening themselves against the ground in a menacing fashion. One had a broken left wing, from a fight or an accident. Both birds kept their beaks open, and moved rhythmically, as if to start the battle again. But as suddenly as it had begun, the fight was over, and the two exhausted birds and the sleek spectator hopped away.

March 16th

Started to paint the lichen with the red spores. I was quite fascinated by its form and colours. Today it is bright but bitterly cold, with the river blown into tiny white horses and driven against the bank. I saw a bird in the reeds with a tiny black head, but it flew away before I could identify it. A couple of partridges flew up in front of me, flying low across the field. Rooks seem to be everywhere at this time of year; there were as many as fifty in the nearby field. And there seems to be a vast population of moles this year, judging by recent activity.

March 18th

I went down to the river well wrapped up as it was a cold day. The willow twigs and young branches were more orange; the ash by the old brick bridge had swollen, dark purplish buds; the May bushes had tiny green closed buds and the pussy willows looked lovely with their pale yellow pollen.

by *Janet Marsh*

March 7
Green woodpecker begins to laugh. Last night I heard that short quick note of birds flying in the dark: if this should be the voice of *Oedicnemus* [stone curlew], as is supposed: then that bird, which is not seen in the dead of winter, is returned. . .

March 8
Mrs Snooke died, aged 86.

The air is soft. Violets blow. Snow lies under hedges. Men plow.

March 9
In the night between the 8th and 9th a vast fragment of an hanger in the parish of Hawkley slipped down; & at the same time several fields below were rifted & torn in a wonderful manner: two houses also & a barn were shattered, a road stopped-up, & some trees thrown down. 50 acres of ground were disordered & damaged by this strange accident. The turf of some pastures was driven into a sort of waves: in some places the ground sunk into hollows.

March 10
Rooks are continually lighting & pulling each other's nests to pieces: these proceedings are inconsistent with living in such close community. And yet if a pair offers to build on a single tree, the nest is plundered & demolished at once. . .

March 12
The golden-crowned wren, *regulus cristalus*, sings. His voice is as minute as his body.

March 16
The cats brought in a dead house-martin from the stable. I was in hopes at first sight that it might have been in a torpid state; but it was decayed, & dry. . .

March 20
We took the tortoise out of its box, & buried it in the garden: but the weather being warm it heaved up the mould, & walked twice down to the bottom of the long walk to survey the premises.

March 21
The tortoise is quite awake, & came-out all day long: toward the evening it buried itself in part.

March 23
A farmer tells me he foresaw this extraordinary weather by the prognostic deportment of his flock; which, when turned-out on a down two or three mornings ago, gamboled & frolicked about like so many lambs.

March 26 & 27
Two sultry days; Mrs Snooke's tortoise came forth out of the ground; but retired again to its hybernaculum in a day or two, & did not appear any more for near a fortnight. Swallows appeared also on the same days, & withdrew again: a strong proof this of their hiding.

March 28
Added about half a pint more of brandy, in all five pints & an half, to the last made-wine, which hisses still pretty much.

by *Gilbert White*

In groups agree:
a) what these two extracts have in common,
b) when you think they were written; what makes you think this,
c) where they are different from each other.

Read these entries from *The Diary of a Teenage Health Freak* by Aidan MacFarlane and Ann McPherson in which personal experiences are shared with a wider audience.

The diary of a teenage health freak

Chapter 7

Learning to Live with my Acne

Tuesday 30th April

Weekend got worse and worse. Pimples have turned into real spots. Every time I looked another had appeared. My skin's gone all greasy, with lumps around my nose. It's disgusting. Dad's sympathetic, but he's not much help. Said, 'Oh, it's just acne. Everyone gets it when they're young.' JUST! That isn't much help to someone with a face covered in molehills. He went on about how they would clear up soon, but they haven't gone yet. Actually they're worse. Tried squeezing them and although I got something out, it's made them flare up. Some seem to have black heads, others have white heads. Maybe I don't wash enough.

Wednesday 1st May

A black day in my life at school. Cilla said, 'Ugh, what have you done to your face?' I thought that would have been obvious. She wears so much make-up, you'd need a spade to find out what was going on on her skin. Called her 'Pancake Face', which hardly improved our relationship. Not that it was much good anyway.

Thursday 2nd May

They're spreading. Slogs was kind enough to point it out to me after games today. Said my back looked like a pizza. Checked in the mirror. He's right. Where are they going to spread to next?

Friday 3rd May

Good old Mum. Thought she hadn't noticed. She left a tube of cream in my room after tea, plus an article she'd found in an old Sunday colour supplement. It's called 'A Spot of Bother' and seems to know what it's talking about.

'*Acne happens most commonly in adolescents because of the surge in hormones that comes with puberty. It tends to be worse in boys (just my luck) and affects the face and shoulders most, because that's where hair follicles are commonest.*
. . . *One thing that you can do for yourself to help your acne is to go out in the sun. Sunlight is good for spots; it reduces the number of bacteria in the skin, encourages peeling (Ugh) to get rid of the horny layer of skin and loosens blackheads, and decreases the rate at which sebum is produced . . .*'

Still don't really understand why I have got them, or what 'sebum' is, but it doesn't sound at all nice.

Saturday 4th May

Aunt Pam's coming tomorrow! Horror. Maybe she won't kiss me now I've got acne. That's the only advantage I can think of. Put the cream on for the second time today. Amazed there's no improvement.

Mum and Dad went out for an hour, leaving me to 'babysit' for Susie, a term she doesn't exactly like. Told her it was exactly right though, as she still spends a lot of time making clothes for her Sindy doll. She'll begin to look like one of them soon. Tried persuading Mum and Dad to pay me. They refused with an argument about how they didn't make me pay for my meals, so offered to go and eat at MacDonalds.

Sunday 5th May

Aunt Pam came and gave me the kiss of Dracula, despite the fact that I'm covered in spots. Hope they

ARE catching. Wonder where I can find out more about acne? Might try the library's dictionary again. Is there a magic cure?

Monday 6th May

Dictionary not much help. Said it was a 'skin eruption with red pimples'. Makes my face sound like a volcano. In despair about the cream I am using. It seems a complete waste of time, but the article said it's worth trying different creams and lotions till you find one that works on your particular skin. Mum's got me this new lotion. Says it's cheaper, and the chemist told her there is no relationship between the cost and whether the treatment works.

Rushed up to the bathroom to try it, as the school disco is in two weeks' time and I'm getting desperate. Embarrassing enough to ask a girl to dance, let alone if you've got acne. It stung a bit when I put it on, so I looked at the instructions to make sure I was doing it right. They were part of a long leaflet which answered most of what I wanted to know.

Apparently 70 per cent of the teenage population have acne at one time or another. It's not a disease but just a normal part of growing up.

Wednesday 22nd May

Even Susie has noticed my spots are a bit better. Just as well, as it's the school disco tonight. I've nearly forgotten what I look like without spots. I don't think my friends would recognize me if they all disappeared. Anyway I'll keep on with the soap even if they do. Noticed today that even Randy Jo has a few spots. Doesn't seem to have put the girls off though. Maybe because most of them have spots too.

Went to the disco. It turned out to be too dark to have to worry about spots. Danced once with Cilla but didn't get anywhere.

I Make a list of everything mentioned here which you would describe as *very private*. Is a diary the only place where such material can be included?

Assignment 26

Keep a diary for a week of your own life.
- Avoid the 'and then' approach which merely lists the repetitive features of your existence.
- Give your diary a particular focus, for example, nature, your family's peculiarities, a strong interest of your own, life in the 1990s.
- Try and find a consistent 'voice' or style for your writing, as in the examples you have read.

Diaries in history

English diary-keeping really began at the end of the sixteenth century, although there are a few examples from earlier times. It became more widespread at the time when growing numbers of people had learned to write for the first time.

Early diaries recorded wars, travel, religious feelings and even the details of running a household. Samuel Pepys is famous throughout the world for his description of the Great Fire of London of 1666. His diaries manage to combine observation of public events with a record of his own more private thoughts.

During the eighteenth century two other major styles of writing also dealt with in this book became commonplace – the letter and the daily newspaper. Many people kept diaries that were intended to be strictly private; some, especially politicians, already began to see the commercial value of the diary. One of the greatest diarists of this time was James Boswell.

> On Wednesday 6 July 1763, Johnson was engaged to sup with me at my lodgings in Downing-Street, Westminster. But on the preceding night my landlord having behaved very rudely to me and some company who were with me, I had resolved not to remain another night in his house. I was exceedingly uneasy at the awkward appearance I supposed I should make to Johnson and the other gentlemen whom I had invited, not being able to receive them at home, and being obliged to order supper at the Mitre. I went to Johnson in the morning, and talked of it as a serious distress. He laughed, and said, 'Consider, Sir, how insignificant this will appear a twelvemonth hence.' — Were this consideration to be applied to most of the little vexatious incidents of life, by which our quiet is too often disturbed, it would prevent many painful sensations. I have tried it frequently, with good effect. 'There is nothing (continued he) in this mighty misfortune; nay, we shall be better at the Mitre.' I told him that I had been at Sir John Fielding's office, complaining of my landlord, and had been informed, that though I had taken my lodgings for a year, I might, upon proof of his bad behaviour, quit them when I pleased, without being under an obligation to pay rent for any longer time than while I possessed them. The fertility of Johnson's

Today we can read about a wide range of public and private subjects. Diaries survive as a means of recording the social changes experienced by each new generation.

Letters, like diaries, are a useful way of recording and sharing personal observations. There are as many styles of letters as there are writers.

Letters

Read this exchange of letters carefully. They are a sample of some correspondence between a visitor to Sri Lanka and a class of 14-year-old students in England.

From: Richard Johnson
Sri Lanka

Dear all,

Hope you're all well. I arrived here safely on 23rd February, early in the morning, to be greeted by intense heat - like a very hot English summer but much more sticky - and the amazing beauty of this place. I presume you've all seen the Bounty advert; well it's similar to that - palm trees, the lot.

I'm working for an organization called Sarvodaya which organizes health programmes, education, youth training schemes, and generally work within each village community. I'm staying in its centre in the village of Baddegama. It's quite a large village, based around a road, with shops and houses along the side of the road. Each shop sells practically everything - bananas, coconuts - to this paper I'm writing on. I'll try to work out a map of the village sometime later, if you would like one.

I'm staying in the centre which is a medium-sized house, which has whitewashed walls, concrete floors and is very open, to keep it cool. My room is shared with an Indonesian bloke called Tegu, who is working here as well. It has a high ceiling, right up to the rafters, where there is a snake apparently, and you can hear the rats squeaking at night. There are two wells, one for washing and one for drinking, however, I still have to put sterilizing chlorine tablets in the drinking water which makes it taste like a swimming-pool, but it's better to be safe than sorry.

The washing well has a bloody great fish in the bottom of it, which tries to climb in the bucket every time you throw it in, which is a great laugh.

The food is very basic: rice three times a day with an assortment of very hot chilli curries each time. Chilli at 8.00am is an interesting experience. You can see the effect of the diet on the people here. They're shorter than an average English person, and thinner. However, this doesn't put them at any disadvantage as their ability to stand the heat (and not sweat) is far greater than mine, and their constitution is far stronger; they're not affected by midget bites, for example, while I'm covered in them.

You could perhaps discuss the difficulties in Asian families adapting to English life-style. That makes me think of something else. Being here you begin to get some understanding of the horrors of racism we get in our country. For example, every single person without exception, stares at me, whispers things behind my back. However, there is a major difference - most of the inquisitive looks are friendly. Imagine what it would be like if the 'staring' was hostile, as it can be in England. Discuss this and let me have your views of the problem, if you think there is one.

My programme of work has not properly started yet. I'm teaching English to various people informally in return for them teaching Sinhala. Learning their language is my number one aim at the moment, as it will make communication a lot easier and also it will distinguish me from tourists who are not liked here. Later on I might be working in a prison and with handicapped people, so I'll tell you about that later.

The poverty here is of course very great, but when you look at the reasons, it is very interesting to see that its causes have direct comparisons (although on a different scale) to those which cause poverty in England. You could perhaps discuss causes of poverty in our country and try to work out how these problems might have counterparts here. There are very rich people here as well of course ...

In future letters I'll tell you more about Buddhism and how it affects people's lives here. I haven't seen enough yet to be able to tell you much about it.

The use of traditional music in the organization I'm working in is also very alive. It consists mainly of excellent fast drumming, which someone has promised to teach me (whether I can or not is a different matter). Also they do a lot of drama based on traditional stories, Buddhist ideas, and old children's folk games. With the cultural director here, I recently translated one of his Sinhalese plays, with footnotes explaining each reference. If you would like a copy of this, I'll send one with my next letter. Apart from the traditional games, the children are mad on cricket and other typical games - football, etc.

The women here play a very subservient role, although they have the chance of education, they eventually end up as wives who spend their lives in the kitchen. They get up earlier than the men, and work all day, and go to bed later than the men. Is this fair? Again look at the comparisons in England.

Although there is free education for everyone here, children still don't go to school for two reasons: i) their parents can't afford the school uniforms; ii) they need to send the children away to work to supplement their income. Can you think of any solutions to these problems? I'll talk more about education later.

I look forward to hearing from you all soon.

Yours

Richard

Richard

Oxfordshire
21st March 1985

Dear Richard

Thank you for your letter; it provoked a great deal of discussion. At first we discussed the letter generally; at the end of the lesson however, we formed into groups to discuss specific topics, the ideas of these groups I will try to collect together here:

On the point about hostility to blacks in our country, people thought that perhaps racist parents were influencing their children and letting them believe that blacks are inferior to whites. Also that young children will pick on any difference that people have to spite them and tease them, therefore, if someone is fat, when in a temper, a child will call them names to do with their fatness, so if the person is black the child will pick on this difference. We thought that TV programmes didn't help the problem of racism. If you watch old films, the blacks are never in the leading roles; they play the parts of faithful servants or workers or even the 'baddy'.

This stereotyping is carried out in to books; in one of Enid Blyton's childrens' books is a character called 'nigger' which could be offensive. We thought that the bad feeling perhaps dated back to the old British Empire when all the 'niggers' and 'little yellow men' were treated as inferior scum, and perhaps older people resent blacks and Asians being treated as equals.

To do with the schooling problems people said that perhaps the wearing of school uniforms should not be made compulsory, or alternatively, the government should provide grants. Somebody suggested that perhaps the children should spend three days a week at school; the rest working. Or perhaps children shouldn't be allowed to work at all under the age of 12. For adult education a night school was suggested.

About the subject of the roles of women, (one which caused a bit of excitement in the female proportion of the class) most of us, boys and girls included, thought that basically the system in Sri Lanka is wrong, however, if the system carries on we thought that the men should give them due credit for what they do. Although the men rule the country it seems that the women do more than their fair share of the work and of course they also have to look after their family. Quoting from one of the girls:

'We don't think women should be 'slaves' any more than blacks should be.'

Another group thought about the problems that immigrants from far away, and with different religions, have in this country. We decided that the dramatic climate change would be most difficult to cope with; Asians would probably find this country cold and damp; the opposite to what you are experiencing. Then, of course, there are the different foods, and, in many cases, a language problem. Also if a sikh child comes to an English school, he might not be able to wear the five K's because it wouldn't tie in with the school uniform. Also in the primary school I went to we were only taught Christian religion and knew nothing of comparative religions. Most of all immigrants would have to put up with racial abuse; this must be very hard, and sometimes affects their chances of getting jobs.

Lastly, there were a few questions people wanted to ask you:

In Sri Lanka, do the children have arranged marriages?
Is there an unemployment problem in Sri Lanka?

We would very much like a translation of a Sinhalese play; we thought perhaps we could act it out.

Thank you very much for writing to us; we hope you are doing well in your job, and we hope to be hearing from you again fairly soon.

Yours,

Class 3B

Class 3B

Sri Lanka

13th April 1985

Dear all,

Thanks a lot for your letter; I was very interested to hear your views. To add to some of the discussions; firstly do you think there is any solution to the racism problem, and if so (I hope you think there is) what is it? Secondly, on the subject of women's rights, what realistic changes can a society make to give women more equality - full-scale revolution, law changes, education - what do you think?

Now to your questions. Firstly arranged marriages: in the majority of cases today marriages are not arranged, however, it is still the traditional method. What are your opinions by the way on this subject? Secondly, unemployment: yes there is a problem. Out of a population of 15m, there are 60,000 people unemployed, which even though it's proportionally less than Britain, it is still very bad. Also there is no 'unemployment benefit'; unemployed people have to rely on friends and family for support. As well as the problem of unemployment, there is also the problem of under-employment, and extremely low wages. Plantation workers and tea estate workers get 24 rupees a day (approx. Rs32 = £1) which is enough to buy 1 1/4 pairs of flip-flops, or nearly 4kg of the lowest grade rice, or just over 1/3 of a sarong (the normal dress for a man here).

The Rs.24 a day is a stable wage, which makes it a little better than the wage of a fisherman, which simply depends upon the catch. The other day I went to a fishing village and helped the men haul in their net on the beach. It took 14 men (and a few kids), 7 on each end of the net, about 3 hours to pull in the net (which is cast the night before). When it finally came ashore there were only 14 medium-sized fish and a small basketful of small ones. At this point a newcomer strolled on to the beach, and started bartering a price for the fish. Eventually he gave them Rs.75 for the small fish, and Rs.85 for all the medium-sized fish. This works out at Rs.160, or just over Rs.11 for each man, for a day's work (30p approx). The man who bought the fish will sell it at Rs.40 per kg, and as there is about 9kg of fish altogether he will make about Rs.200 profit - a lot of money for walking on to the beach. I have my opinions of what should happen here, please tell me yours. Should it just be accepted as it is? Also at first sight you might think 'this sort of thing doesn't happen in Britain', but look hard and I'm sure you'll see some interesting comparisons.

The majority of people here are Sinhalese Buddhists, and it is them that I'm staying with. Through a series of lucky chances I've managed to start working with the Buddhist monks (with the saffron robes and shaved heads) at the local temple. They're a great bunch, and although they are very religious people, they're also very normal. The one monk I stay with is a great laugh (funny expression for a monk but it's true); he jokes and chats with me like any normal person.

Yours Richard

Describe your impression of life in Sri Lanka as portrayed by Richard. How accurate a picture of any country do you think it is possible to give in a letter? Find out more about anything here which interests you.

▼ Assignment 27

Correspond with someone you do not know who lives in another part of the world. Describe your life and respond to her/his letters. You could make a link with a school in another part of Britain or in another country or you could arrange something independently.

Special feature

Computers don't argue

Tell the story of these letters as simply and amusingly as you can.

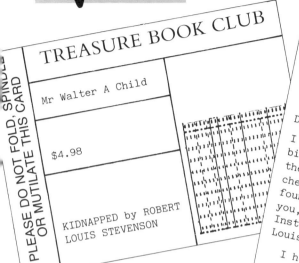

TREASURE BOOK CLUB

PLEASE DO NOT FOLD, SPINDLE OR MUTILATE THIS CARD

Mr Walter A Child

$4.98

KIDNAPPED by ROBERT LOUIS STEVENSON

---

437 Woodlawn Drive
Panduk, Michigan
16 November 1965

Treasure Book Club
1823 Mandy Street
Chicago, Illinois

Dear Sirs,

I wrote you recently about the computer punch card you sent, billing me for Kim, by Rudyard Kipling. I did not open the package containing it until I had already mailed you my cheque for the amount on the card. On opening the package, I found the book missing half its pages. I sent it back to you, requesting either another copy or my money back. Instead you have sent me a copy of Kidnapped by Robert Louis Stevenson. Will you please straighten this out?
I hearby return the copy of Kidnapped.

Sincerely yours,
Walter A Child
Walter A Child

Dear Sirs,

May I direct your attention to my letter of 16 November 1965? You are still continuing to dun me with computer punch cards for a book I did not order. Whereas, actually, it is your company that owes me money.

Sincerely yours,
Walter A Child
Walter A Child

TREASURE BOOK CLUB
1823 Mandy Street
Chicago, Illinois

1 February 1966
Mr Walter A Child
437 Woodlawn Drive
Panduk, Michigan

Dear Mr Child,
We have sent you a number of reminders concerning an amount owing us as a result of a book purchase you have made from us. This amount which is $4.98 is now long overdue.
This situation is disappointing to us, particularly since there was no hesitation on our part in extending you credit at the time original arrangements for these purchases were made by you. If we do not receive payment in full by return mail, we will be forced to turn the matter over to a collection agency.

Very truly yours,
Samuel P. Grimes
Samuel P Grimes

5 February 1966
Dear Mr Grimes

Will you stop sending me punch cards and form letters and make me some kind of a direct answer from a human being?

I don't owe you money. You owe me money. Maybe I should turn your company over to a collection agency.

Walter A Child

Walter A Child

— FEDERAL COLLECTION OUTFIT —
88 Prince Street, Chicago, Illinois

28 February 1966

Mr Walter A Child
437 Woodlawn Drive
Panduk, Michigan

Dear Mr Child,
Your account with the TREASURE BOOK CLUB of $4.98 plus interest and charges has been turned over to our agency for collection. The amount now due is $6.83. Please send your cheque for this amount or we shall be forced to take immediate action.

Jacob N Harshe

Ja

Maloney, Maloney, MacNamara and Pruit
ATTORNEYS

89 Prince Street
Chicago, Illinois

Mr Walter A Child
437 Woodlawn Drive
Panduk, Michigan

29th April 1966

Dear Mr Child
Your indebtedness to the Treasure Book Club has been referred to us for legal action to collect.

This indebtedness is now in the amount of $10.01. If you will send us this amount so that we may receive it before 5th May 1966, the matter may be satisfied. However, if we do not receive satisfaction in full by that date, we will take steps to collect through the courts.

I am sure you will see the advantage of avoiding a judgement against you, which as a matter of record would do lasting harm to your credit rating.

Very truly yours,

Hagthorpe M Pruit Jr.

Hagthorpe M Pruit, Jr
Attorney at Law

— FEDERAL COLLECTION OUTFIT —
88 Prince Street, Chicago, Illinois

8 April 1966

Mr Walter A Child
437 Woodlawn Drive
Panduk, Michigan

Dear Mr Child
You have seen fit to ignore our courteous requests to settle your long overdue account with TREASURE BOOK CLUB, which is now, with accumulated interest and charges in the amount of $7.51.
If payment in full is not forthcoming by 11 APRIL 1966 we will be forced to turn the matter to our attorneys for immediate court action.

Jacob N Harshe

Jacob N Harshe

Dear Mr Pruit

You don't know what a pleasure it is to me in this matter to get a letter from a live human being to whom I can explain the situation.

The whole matter is silly, I explained it fully in my letters to the Treasure Book Company. But I might as well have been trying to explain to the computer that puts out their punch cards, for all the good it seemed to do. Briefly, what happened was I ordered a copy of Kim by Rudyard Kipling for $4.98. When I opened the package they sent me, I found the book had only half its pages, but I'd previously mailed a cheque to pay them for the book.

I sent the book back to them, asking either for a whole copy or my money back. Instead, they sent me a copy of Kidnapped by Robert Louis Stevenson – which I had not ordered; and for which they have been trying to collect from me.

Meanwhile, I am still waiting for the money back that they owe me for the copy of Kim that I didn't get. That's the whole story. Maybe you can help me straighten them out.

Relieved yours,

Walter A Child

Walter A Child

PS I also sent them back their copy of Kidnapped as soon as I got it but it didn't seem to help. They have never even acknowledged.

Maloney, Maloney, MacNamara and Pruit ATTORNEYS

89 Prince Street
Chicago, Illinois

Mr Walter A Child
437 Woodlawn Drive
Panduk, Michigan

9th May 1966

Dear Mr Child

I am in possession of no information indicating that any item purchased by you from the Treasure Book Club has been returned.

I would hardly think that, if the case had been as you stated the Treasure Book Club would have retained us to collect the amount owing from you.

If I do not receive your payment in full within three days, by 12 May 1966, we will be forced to take legal action.

Very truly yours

Hagthorpe M Pruit Jr.

Hagthorpe M Pruit, Jr

---

437 Woodlawn Drive
Panduk, Michigan

31 May 1966

Samuel P Grimes
Vice President, Treasure Book Club
1823 Mandy Street
Chicago, Illinois

Grimes,

This business has gone far enough. I've got to come down to Chicago on business of my own tomorrow. I'll see you then and we'll get this straightened out once and for all, about who owes what to whom, and how much!

Yours,

Walter A Child

Walter A Child

Court of Minor Claims CHICAGO, ILLINOIS

Name WALTER A. CHILD	Address 437 WOODLAWN
DRIVE, PANDUK,	MICHIGAN

Be informed that a judgement was taken and entered against you in this court this day of 26 MAY 1966 in the amount of $15.55 Including court costs.

Payment in satisfaction of this judgement may be made to this court or to the adju~~~~ed creditor. In the case of payment being made ~~~~~ with this court in order obtained from the cr~~~~ ~~~~tion with this to free you of legal ~~~~~ judgement.

Court of Minor Claims

Judgment was passed this day of
27 May 1966
under
Statute $15.66
Against Walter A Child
of 347 Woodlawn Drive
Panduk, Michigan
Pray to enter a duplicate claim
for judgement
For amount Statute 941

PICAYUNE COURT From the desk of the clerk

Harry,
The attached computer card from the Chicago's Minor Claims Court against A. Walter has a 1500-series statute number on it. That puts it over in Criminal with you, rather than in Civil, with me. So I herewith submit it for your computer instead of mine. How's business?

Joe

CRIMINAL RECORDS PANDUK MICHIGAN

Convicted: (Child) A Walter
On: 26 May 1966
Address: 437 Woodlawn Drive Panduk, Michigan
Crim: Statute 1566 (corrected) 1567
Crime: Kidnap
Date: 16 November 1965
Notes: At large. To be picked up at once.

POLICE DEPARTMENT, PANDUK, MICHIGAN

TO POLICE DEPARTMENT, CHICAGO, ILLINOIS

CONVICTED SUBJECT A. (Complete first name unknown) Walter, sought here in connection ref. your notification of judgement for kidnap of child named Robert Louis Stevenson on 16 November 1965 Information here indicates subject fled his residence at 437 Woodlawn Drive, Panduk, and may be again in your area.

Possible contact in your area

The Treasure Book Club, 1823 Mandy Street, Chicago, Illinois. Subject not known to be dangerous. Pick up and hold, advising us of capture...

NOTES

To Police Department, Panduk, Michigan

Reference your request to pick up and hold A (complete first name unknown) Walter, wanted in Panduk on Statute 1567, crime of kidnapping.

Subject arrested at offices of Treasure Book Club, operating there under alias ~~Anthony~~ Walter Anthony Child and attempting to collect $4.98 from one Samuel. P. Grimes, employee of that company — HOLDING FOR YOUR ADVICE

POLICE DEPARTMENT, PANDUK, MICHIGAN

TO POLICE DEPARTMENT, CHICAGO, ILLINOIS

Ref: A Walter (Alias Walter Anthony Child) subject wanted for crime of kidnap, your ref: your computer punch card notification of judgement, dated 27 May 1966. Copy our criminal records punch card herewith forwarded to your computer section.

NAL RECORDS CHICAGO, ILLINOIS

Subject: Correction omitted record supplied

Applicable Statute No: 1567

Judgement No: 456789

Trial Record: Apparently misfiled and unavailable

Direction: To appear for sentencing before Judge John Alexander Mc Divat, Courtroom A 9 June 1966

From the desk of Judge Alexander J. McDivot

2 June 1966

Dear Tony

I've got an adjudged criminal coming up before me for sentencing Thursday morning – but the trial transcript is apparently misfiled. I need some kind of information (Ref. A. Walter – Judgement No. 456789, Criminal). For example, victim harmed?

Jack Mc Divot

Jack Mc Divot

REQUEST

RECORDS SEARCH UNIT

Re: Ref. Judgement No. 456789 was victim harmed?

Tonio Malagasi
Records Division

To; Records Search Unit
    Criminal Records Division
    Police Department
    Chicago, Illinois

Subject: Your query re Robert Louis Stevenson
         File no. 1896230

Action: Subject deceased. Age at death 44yrs.
        Futher information requested?

RECORDS SEARCH UNIT/CRIMINAL RECORDS DIVISION
POLICE DEPARTMENT
CHICAGO, ILL

To Statistics Office June 6 1966
Attn. Information Division
Subject:RE File No 1896230
NO FURTHER INFORMATION REQUIRED

---

une 1966

   Judge Alexander J McDivot's chamber

r Jack,   Ref: Judgement No 456789

e victim in this kidnap case was apparently slain.

From the strange lack of background information
the killer and his victim, as well as the victim's
e, this smells to me like a gangland killing.
is is for your information. Don't quote me. It
ems to me, though, that Stevenson - the victim -
as a name that rings a faint bell with me.
ossibly one of the East Coast Mob, since the
ssociation comes back to me as something about
irates - possibly New York dockage hijackers -
nd something about buried loot.

   As I say, above is only speculation for your
rivate guidance.

   Any time I can help...

Best
Tony
Tony Malagasi
Records Division

RECORDS SEARCH UNIT/CRIMINAL RECORDS DIVISION
POLICE DEPARTMENT
CHICAGO, ILL

7 June 1966

To: Tonio Malagasi, Records Division

Re: Ref: Judgement No 456789 - victim
    is dead.

---

49 Water Street, Chicago, Illinois

MICHAEL R. REYNOLDS
Attorney at Law

8 June 1966

Dear Tim,

Regret, I can't make the fishing trip. I've been court-appointed
here to represent a man about to be sentenced tomorrow on a
kidnapping charge.

   Ordinarily, I might have tried to beg off, and Mc Divot, who is
doing the sentencing, would probably have turned me loose. But this
is the damdnest thing you ever heard of.

   The man being sentenced has apparently been not only charged, but
adjudged guilty as a result of a comedy of errors too long to go
into here. He not only isn't guilty - he's got the best case I
ever heard of for damages against one of the larger Book Clubs
headquartered here in Chicago. And that's a case I wouldn't mind
taking on.

   It's inconceivable - but damnably possible, once you stop to
think of it in this day and age of machine-made records - that a
completely innocent man could be put in this position.

   There shouldn't be much to it. I've asked to see McDivot tomorrow
before the time for sentencing, and it'll just be a matter of
explaining to him. Then I can discuss the damage suit with my
freed client at his leisure.

Fishing next weekend?

   Yours,

   Mike

10 June

Dear Tim

In haste –
No fishing this coming week either I'm afraid. Sorry.
You won't believe it. My innocent-as-a-lamb-and-I'm-not-kidding
client has just been sentenced to death for first-degree murder in
connection with the death of his kidnap victim.
Yes, I explained the whole thing to Mc Divot. And when he
explained his situation to me I nearly fell out of my chair.
It wasn't a matter of my not convincing him. It took less than
three minutes to show him that my client should never have been
within the walls of the County Jail for a second. But – get this –
Mc Divot couldn't do a thing about it.
The point is my man has already been judged guilty according to
the computerized records. In the absence of a trial record – of
course there never was one –(but that's something I'm not free to
explain to you now) – the judge has to go by what records are
available. And in the case of an adjudged prisoner, McDivot's
only legal choice was whether to sentence to life imprisonment or
execution.
The death of the kidnap victim, according to the statute, made
the death penalty mandatory. Under the new laws governing length
of time for appeal, which has been shortened because of the new
system of computerized records, to force the elimination of
unfair delay and mental anguish to those condemned, I have five
days in which to file an appeal, and ten to have it acted on.
Needless to say, I'm not going to monkey with an appeal. I'm
going directly to the Governor for a pardon – after which we will
get this farce reversed. Mc Divot has already written the Governor
also, explaining that his sentence was ridiculous, but that he had
no choice. Between the two of us, we ought to have a pardon in
short order.
Then I'll make the fur fly...
And we'll get in some fishing.

Best

27 June 1966
Michael Reynolds
49 Water Street
Chicago Illinois

Dear Mike,
Where is that pardon?
My execution date is only five
days from now!
Walt

To: Michael R Reynolds,

Dear Mr Reynolds,
In reply to your query about the request for
pardon for Walter A Child (A. Walter), may I
inform you that the governor is still on his
trip with the Midwest Governors Committee,
examining the wall in Berlin. He should be
back next Friday.
I will bring your request and letters to his
attention to him the minute he returns.

Clara B. Gilkes
Clara B Gilkes
Secretary to the Governor

...ld (A. Walter)
...ck E
...Illinois State Penitentiary
Joliet, Illinois

Dear Walt,

The Governor returned, but was called away immediately to the
White House in Washington to give his views on inter-state sewage.
I am camping on his doorstep and will be on him the moment he
arrives here.
Meanwhile, I agree with you about the seriousness of the
situation. The warden at the prison there, Mr Allen Magruder
will bring this letter to you and have a private talk to you. I
urge you to listen to what he has to say; and I enclose letters
from your family also urging you to listen to Warden Magruder.

Yours,

Mike

chael R Reynolds
Water Street
icago, Illinois

ear Mike,

This letter is being smuggled out by warden Magruder)

As I was talking to warden Magruder in my cell here, news
was brought to him that the Governor was at last
returning for a while to Illinois, and will be in his office
early tomorrow morning, Friday. So you will have time to
stop my execution on Saturday.

Accordingly, I have turned down the Warden's kind
offer of a chance to escape: since he told me that he
could by no means guarantee to have all the guards
out of the way when I tried it; and there was a chance
of my being killed escaping. But now everything will
straighten itself out. Actually an experience as fantastic
as this had to breakdown sometime under its own weight.

Best, Walt,

Failure to route document properly

To: GOVERNOR HUBERT DANIEL WILLIKENS

Re: Pardon issued to Walter A Child, 1 July 1966

Dear State Employee:

You have failed to submit your Routing number
Please resubmit document with this card and form 876,
explaining your authority for placing a TOP RUSH
category on this document. Form 876 must be signed
by your departmental superior.

Resubmit on:

Resubmit on - earliest possible date
ROUTING SERVICE office is open. In this case,
Tuesday 5 July 1966.

WARNING: Failure to submit form 876 WITH THE
SIGNATURE OF YOUR SUPERIOR may make
you liable to prosecution for misusing a Service of
State Government. A warrant may be issued for
your arrest.

There are **NO** exceptions.
YOU have been **WARNED**.

UBERT DANIEL WILLIKENS , Governor of the State of
nois, and invested with the authority and powers
pertaining thereto, including the power to pardon those in
y judgement wrongfully convicted or otherwise deserving
executive mercy, do this day of 1 JULY 1966
nnounce and proclaim that WALTER A CHILD
A. WALTER) now in custody as a consequence of
erroneous conviction upon a crime of which he is entirely
innocent, is fully and freely pardoned of said crime. And I
do direct the necessary authorities having custody of the
said WALTER A CHILD (A. WALTER) in whatever place
or places he may be held, to immediately free, release,
and allow unhindered departure to him . . . .

Interdepartmental Routing Service

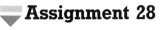 **Assignment 28**   Write an amusing or similar series of letters, etc. of your own. Use the letters to tell
your story for you.

Develop your 'story' out of an apparently insignificant beginning like the Book
Club mix-up above.

The great train robbery

On Friday 2 August, five days before the robbery was due to take place, Gordon Goody flew to Belfast with his mother and a friend. They stayed in Lisburn with his uncle and Gordon went to some lengths to make his presence noticed: he faked a fight in a pub, and had the publican call the police, but this stratagem failed because they could not be bothered to come out.

On Saturday 3 August, Roger Cordrey went to the house of some acquaintances in Oxford to ask if he could rent a room on the following Tuesday. They had no room, but they promised to find him somewhere, so he returned to Brighton to find that his wife had left him. For some months they had been getting on badly together, largely because he spent so much time away from home; and while feeling neglected, she had

been befriended by another man. Now she had gone, leaving the youngest child with an old lady next door.

Roger was depressed by his wife's flight – the more so because he felt himself to blame – and it destroyed any pleasure he might have taken in the final preparation of his equipment. He went up to London on the morning of Monday 5 August, stayed with his mother in Hampton Court, and went to bed early.

He was woken at eleven by the telephone. The old lady in Brighton who was looking after his son had had a heart attack and Roger was told that someone must fetch the child. He got dressed, telephoned some friends to see if they knew where his wife could be, but was unable to trace her. He had no alternative but to drive down to Brighton in his car, fetch his son and drive him back to London. By the time he got back to Hampton Court early in the morning, Roger was totally exhausted.

The same day Roy had driven out to London Airport in his Mini Cooper with Jim Hussey to meet the German sent by Karl to look after his interests. They were equipped with a photograph and picked him out as he came through passport control – a tall, well-dressed man with fair hair and a crocodile brief-case who gave his name as Sigi. He said little as they drove back into London to stay with Jim in his parents' flat.

On the morning of Tuesday 6 August, the whole gang prepared to move. Bruce and John despatched their wives and children to stay with Jimmy White's wife in their caravan in Winchelsea and then set off in the old Land Rover to pick up Ronnie Biggs and old Stan who had told their wives that they were going on a tree-felling job in Wiltshire. They reached Leatherslade Farm in time for lunch, and since the stores were already there they lit the stove and cooked themselves something to eat. Afterwards they changed into white overalls, and while Ronnie and John stayed in the house, Bruce went into the garden to see where they could dig a pit to bury the mail-bags. Old Stan sat on a deck-chair taking the sun.

From the fields behind the farm, a man appeared who introduced himself to Bruce as Mr Wyatt, a neighbouring farmer, and said that he would like to continue the arrangement whereby he had rented a field from the previous owners, the Rixons. Bruce said that he was not the owner, but only the decorator.

'Who is the owner, then?' asked Mr Wyatt.

'Mr Fielding from Aylesbury,' said Bruce.

Mr Wyatt departed, and a little later Jimmy White and his friend Alf Thomas arrived with the lorry. They backed it into the shed and then took the Land Rover to return to London. There they crossed the Thames and picked up Frank Munroe, Tommy Wisbey and Bob Welch who all piled into the back with their sleeping bags and drove on to fetch Roger at Hampton Court. He appeared looking exhausted, with a kit bag and three empty suitcases for his money. He also wheeled out a bicycle: there was complaints from the others, but Roger insisted on taking his bike and they could hardly leave without him.

Half-way to Leatherslade Farm, they stopped for petrol and while the tank was being filled, a little boy wrote down their registration number in his notebook which caused some anxiety because Jimmy White had given the stolen Land Rover the same number as the one they had bought; since the police could check numbers against makes, it seemed sensible to use the legitimate registration.

When they reached the entrance to the track leading up to the farm, Alf leapt out to open the gate; it was now late in the afternoon and they could hear the sound of the milking machinery in the cow-shed. They drove up to the farm to find that Roy, dressed like a local farmer in old tweeds and a cloth cap, had already arrived in the other Land Rover with Charlie, Buster, Bill, Jim Hussey and the strange German in a smart suit.

Jimmy White now began to skin and cook a rabbit they had run over on the road. The others started blowing up their air-mattresses and laying claim to corners of the four bedrooms, one of which was reserved for Sigi whom Jim had been told to keep out of the way. Bruce came up to explain to him that while they were at the track, he was to remain at the farm; and if for any reason they did not return, he was to change into a pair of *Lederhosen* which Bruce had brought to the farm, and make his escape as a tourist on Roger's bike.

While Sigi remained in an upstairs room, the other stranger, old Stan, shuffled around from room to room, sucking his pipe and smiling. None of the thieves apart from Bruce, Buster and Ronnie Biggs had ever seen him before, and the sight of his beaming, gullible face confirmed their worst fears. Quite clearly he had little idea of what was going on, and if anything went wrong and he fell into the hands of the police he could identify every one of them. They tried to avoid him, and every time he entered one room, they would sneak out of it with averted faces. Occasionally he would corner one of them and say, 'What's your name, son?' 'Joe Bloggs,' would come the answer, or 'Elvis Presley'. Later Bruce told Ronnie that Stan had to be kept out of the way, so Ronnie took him up to a bedroom and left him there. When the rabbit was ready, Ronnie took a plate up to him: the others ate it downstairs. When Jimmy White handed a plate to Tommy Wisbey, he noticed that he was not wearing gloves.

'Put your gloves on, Tom,' he said.

'Oh yeah,' said Tommy, reaching into his pocket for them.

Only one member of the gang was missing – Gordon. By Wednesday morning he had still not arrived. No one was particularly anxious, but Bruce was always irritated by Gordon's independent ways, and became increasingly angry as the day wore on. The others were growing nervous in anticipation of the night's work, and Buster handed out pep pills to those who wanted them. Some dozed on their air-mattresses; others played Monopoly, or made sure that their uniforms fitted them, and checked their equipment – their masks, gloves, coshes and pick-axe handles. Buster had the same type of pipe-spring cosh as he had used on the Airport Robbery. Jim Hussey's was a length of lead piping with a leather strap; Charlie's a length of copper cable. Some of them had prepared balaclava helmets to disguise their faces; others had stocking masks; and one had a black hood with holes cut out for his eyes. They all had gloves. Buster's were leather with string backs; Roy's were made of wool; Jim Hussey's of black velvet.

Old Stan, of course, had neither cosh nor mask though since he was to drive the train Ronnie had made sure he had gloves. Nor did he wear a soldier's uniform. Roger too remained in a scruffy old jacket and trousers which he had carefully searched for anything which might identify him. He had a spare set of clothes in a suitcase upstairs. He was bored, depressed and very tired. He had hardly slept on his air-mattress the night before and was still worrying about his wife. Moreover Buster and Bruce had told him that morning that he could only leave the farm with the rest of them on the Sunday after the robbery. They had put it gently, but he knew they meant what they said. Late in the afternoon he felt so exhausted that he was afraid he might doze off on the job, so he took a sleeping pill and went upstairs.

They stayed in the farmhouse for fear of being seen. Jimmy White was allowed out with Ronnie Biggs to change the plates of the lorry and the Land Rovers from civilian to military numbers and stick on the square, regimental emblems. Then, as it started to get dark, they saw a Jaguar stop at the foot of the lane. Out stepped Gordon Goody.

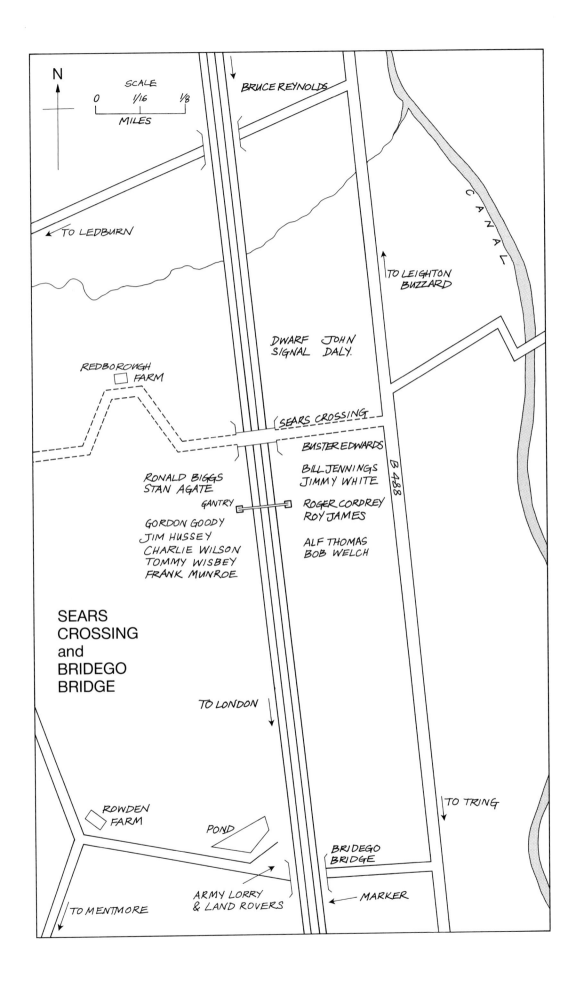

N

SCALE
0   1/16   1/8
MILES

BRUCE REYNOLDS

← TO LEDBURN

C A N A L

TO LEIGHTON
BUZZARD

DWARF   JOHN
SIGNAL   DALY.

REDBOROUGH
☐ FARM

SEARS CROSSING

BUSTER EDWARDS

BILL JENNINGS
JIMMY WHITE

RONALD BIGGS
STAN AGATE

GANTRY

ROGER CORDREY
ROY JAMES

GORDON GOODY
JIM HUSSEY
CHARLIE WILSON
TOMMY WISBEY
FRANK MUNROE

ALF THOMAS
BOB WELCH

B 488

SEARS
CROSSING
and
BRIDEGO
BRIDGE

TO LONDON

TO TRING

ROWDEN
FARM

POND

BRIDEGO
BRIDGE

ARMY LORRY
& LAND ROVERS

MARKER

← TO MENTMORE

1 Make a list of all the train robbers mentioned in this extract.

2 Make brief notes about each member of the gang based on what the author of this biography has chosen to write about.

Example

Name	Comment
Roger Cordrey	Unhappily married. Wife recently left him. Youngest son looked after by his mother in Hampton Court during robbery. Very upset by family sit.

3 In groups, make up the conversation that might have taken place in the 'old landrover' on Tuesday 6 August between the four men, including Ronnie Biggs. Include details such as the excuses each man had given his family.

4 In groups, talk about the two moments in this piece when unexpected events occurred which threatened the gang and which might later have been useful evidence for the police.

5 Imagine the robbery has now happened. Use the information here to prepare a brief radio news flash, including descriptions of the gang which might lead to their arrest.

6 Using the map on page 123 to help you to continue the story as it *might* have happened describe the train robbery itself. Make use of the information you have which suggests possible tensions between some members of the gang.

7 Talk about whether you think book and films should be made about known criminals.

8 Read some other examples of biographical writing. For example, you could find out about Marilyn Monroe, John Lennon, Winnie Mandela, Martin Luther King, Winston Churchill, Charlie Chaplin, Judi Dench.

▼ Assignment 29

Write a short biographical piece describing part of the life of someone you admire. She or he could be alive or dead, well- or little-known. Research your subject carefully. Try and focus on a period of time or an activity which has particular interest and would make someone want to read your writing.

Love and sex are tricky for Little Old Ladies

FIRST PERSON

ARE you little, 60 and female? If so, you qualify – as I have just done – as a Little Old Lady. Everyone who is younger (which seems to be most people) knows exactly what Little Old Ladies are like. For instance, it is well known that we're always in a muddle.

When we go to the supermarket we can never find what we want and we can never find an assistant who can tell us. So we spend a lot of time wandering about, banging into other people's trollies. We then hold up the queue at the till while we fumble with plastic bags and get tangled up in the handles of our shopping-trollies. If we are trying to be really up to date and paying by cheque, the cheque-card will be under layers of pension-books, travel-permits, cheap matineé tickets and various types of specs.

Our incompetence is known to be bottomless, indoors and out. If we attempt to knit we will drop about a quarter of our stitches, and turn out square purple garments everyone is too embarrassed to wear. If we venture on a short holiday, we are sure to be using last year's timetable, and the train we ask our children to meet no longer exists. And as we have no idea what a telephonecard is, or where you'd get one, we can't ring from the station to tell them the train is tomorrow after all.

Indeed, the entire modern age is quite beyond the Little Old Lady. None of us could possibly work a video, or even be quite sure what a video is. And if some kind relation has given us a tape-recorder, we have no notion how to change the tape, or what to ask for when we need a new one. So the original tape eventually shreds into little bits which jam the machine, and it has to be hidden when the kind relation comes to stay.

So long as washing-machines are fairly basic we can be trusted with them, because they were around, in a primitive form, in the days when we were still young and competent. Even so we must have the instructions handy, for frequent consultation on which of the 24 electronic programmes we must use for what. Little Old Ladies have been heard mutter that it would be simpler to do the washing in a river.

We can usually manage the basic knobs on the TV, and we're all right with the wireless so long as it's got only Long and Medium wave. VHF and FM are, of course, quite beyond us, and as for K. Herz — we always thought that was a car-hire firm, or perhaps an American novelist.

Alcohol is known to be a problem area for Little Old Ladies. For a start, we're all suspected of being secret drinkers of cheap sherry. At a meal we're expected to prefer sweet white wine to vintage burgundy – and not much of that either. At parties we're asked if we'd prefer tomato-juice. If we stand our ground, and go on repeating 'Gin and Tonic' often enough, we will be given half a teaspoonful of gin in a quarter of pint of tonic, because it's well known that we have weak heads.

And our public expects that because of our extreme old age we'll want to leave the party early. If we are still thought safe driving our own cars, we are sped on our way at 10.30 with anxious exhortations to drive carefully. If we have no car we are committed to the care of a cab-driver, and asked if we have enough money for the fare.

Which brings me to the subject of driving. Whenever the car ahead is travelling at 20 miles an hour on the crown of the road; whenever someone opens a car door in the path of your own advancing vehicle; whenever a car signalling left turns abruptly right under the bonnet of an advancing juggernaut – then you can be sure the driver is a Little Old Lady. And, as everyone knows, we don't understand what the hard shoulder of a motorway is for, so we tend to use it for a little peaceful motoring when everyone else is going too fast.

Love and sex is another tricky area for Little Old Ladies. Clearly a Little Old Lady could never have fallen in love – and still less could anyone ever have fallen in love with *her* – because all Little Old Ladies are known to be semi-virginal, extremely ignorant, and very against sex. If she has had children, then obviously occasional sex has been forced upon her, but it's not considered suitable for her to refer to *it*.

She may be allowed to make occasional comments about the great romantic moments of her life, but she mustn't do this too often, or with too much relish. And at her age a Little Old Lady is certainly not expected to fall in love, because, in someone so old, falling in love is comic and embarrassing. She may be allowed to marry, if the arrangement seems suitable and convenient, and everyone is consulted, but things must not get soppy or out of hand.

It's thought to be quite sweet if she holds hands with her elderly gentleman friend, but that is definitely as far as things should go. If she wants any more than this, the Little Old Lady must draw her curtains, or leave the country.

All Little Old Ladies are meant to enjoy coffee-mornings with other old folk. If we don't, we are definitely difficult and may have to go to a Home. A newly-qualified Little Old Lady is used to being among the oldest in her household, then she suddenly finds, at the Old Folks' Coffee Morning, that she's a mere girl, a debutante.

In fact, all social life can be a problem for Little Old Ladies. Unless we happen to catch a glimpse in a mirror, we can all too easily forget – in the general excitement of food and conversation – that we're old at all. A surprise look on the faces of our younger companions will remind us we're not playing the part expected. For instance, it's thought to be very tiresome for a Little Old Lady to actually *know* about anything. She must never be noisy or opinionated and is certainly not expected to have views on controversial topics such as Aids or abortion, or the SDP (though she may, if she so wishes, express opinions on roses, soft furnishings, or the Queen's hats).

It is, of course, accepted that Little Old Ladies never know what the date is, always forget the shopping-list, can never remember the cost of second-class stamps, lose their specs a dozen times a day, and can't recollect either the title or the author of the book they have just put down. And because being so old is very tiring I must now take my afternoon rest. In fact, I'd better lie down before I forget what I came upstairs for.

Sheila Sullivan
The Guardian

125

Man bit off budgie's head in restaurant

A MAN WHO bit off a budgerigar's head in a restaurant was fined £100 with £15 costs yesterday. John Farley, 36, decapitated the bird, Beauty, with a single bite while he was dining with friends in Lydney, Gloucestershire, last October. He pleaded guilty at Lydney Magistrates' Court to a charge of causing criminal damage.

Michael Davies, for the prosecution, said John Higgins and his girlfriend arrived at the restaurant with his mother's budgerigar and had joined Farley. The bird was flying about freely and landed on them and other customers.

Farley kept asking for the bird and at one stage caught hold of it and squeezed it. But it flew away. Suddenly he grabbed it again, Mr Davies added. 'He put it into his mouth and bit off its head in one bite.'

Mr Higgins and his girlfriend were extremely upset and reported the matter to the RSPCA, but the society could not take any action because there was no evidence the bird had suffered, as it had died instantly.

Gwyn James, for the defence, said it was a bizarre situation in which someone had taken a budgie to a crowded public restaurant, and the resulting incident could not be regarded as other than a stupid and silly act.

▼Assignment 30

After reading these offbeat approaches to what makes news, write your own unusual article for a newspaper.

Possible suggestions

- A report of a highly-unusual incident in a public place which led to a court case.
- An article exploring the real-life of another stereotype, other than 'the little old lady'.

Index of assignments

*Particularly suitable assignment to be undertaken in controlled conditions.

Acknowledgements

The Editor and Publishers gratefully acknowledge permission to reproduce copyright material in this book.

Autobiography

BOB GELDOF: from *Is That It?*, (Sidgwick & Jackson, 1986), by permission of the publishers. MOHAMMED ELBAJA: from 'My Life', Mayanke Patel from 'Rare Bengal Tiger', JOHN HAWKRIDGE: from 'Home from Home', all in *Our Lives* (1979), by permission of The English Centre. WINIFRED FOLEY: from *A Child in the Forest*, (Century), by permission of the publishers. JOHN GUILGUD: from *An Actor and His Time*, (Sidgwick & Jackson, 1979), by permission of the publishers. LAURIE LEE: from *Cider with Rosie*, (The Hogarth Press, 1959), by permission of the publishers. ROALD DAHL: from *Tales from Childhood: Boy*, (Jonathan Cape, 1984 and Penguin books), © Roald Dahl 1984, by permission of Murray Pollinger, agents. LYNNE JONES: from *Keeping the Peace*, (Women's Press), by permission of the publishers.

Interests and Beliefs

JOHN and SALLY SEYMOUR: from *Self Sufficiency*, (Faber & Faber), by permission of the publishers. Extract from GILLIE & MERCER: *The Sunday Times New Book of Body Maintenance*, by permission of Michael Joseph Ltd. Extract from 'A Smoker's Guide to Giving Up', (Health Education Authority leaflet), by permission of the Authority. PARAMJIT KAUR: from *Bitter Sweet Dreams*, (Virago, 1987), by permission of the author and publishers. GABY WATERS: from *Science Surprises*, (Usborne, 1985), by permission of the publishers.

Arguing a Case

TANYA NYARI: from 'The Abuse of Animals', DOMINIQUE WALKER: from 'Private Education', both in *Say What You Think*, (1985), by permission of the English Centre.

Newspapers and Magazines

MARTIN WAINWRIGHT: article from *The Guardian* (11 October 1986), and JAMES ERLICHMAN: article from *The Guardian* (November 1986), both by permission of the authors and Guardian Newspapers Ltd. CLIVE EDWARDS: article from *The Independent* (4 August 1987), and PETER WILBY: article from *The Independent* (6 November 1987), both by permission of Newspaper Publishing plc. DAWN DOHERTY: article from *The Oxford Times* (16 January 1987), by permission of Oxford and County Newspapers. SUE FOX: article from *The Sunday Times Magazine* (25 October 1987), FIONA CONNELLY: article from *The Sunday Times Magazine* (July 1987) and DEBRA McARTHUR: article from *The Sunday Times Magazine* (March 1988), all by permission of the authors, the interviewees and Times Newspapers Ltd. JOHN BALDING: Research charts (Exeter University HEA Schools Education Unit, 1987), by permission of J.W. Balding.

Publicity Material

Extract from publicity leaflet by permission of The Children's Legal Centre. Extract from leaflet 'What to do About Glue-Sniffing', by permission of the Health Education Authority. Extract from leaflet 'Are Animal Experiments Necessary for Cosmetic Products', by permission of the Research Defence Society. One page advertisement by permission of The National Anti-Vivisection Society. Information leaflet by permission of The Samaritans. B. AVISON: from *How To Complain*, (Longman, 1986), by permission of the publishers.

The Natural World

COLIN SHAWYER and PETER BANKS: from 'Barn Owls on the Brink', in *The New Scientist* (17 December 1987), and FRED PEARCE: from 'A History of Assault by Acid Rain', in *The New Scientist* (5 November 1987), the weekly review of science and technology, both by permission of New Scientist Syndication. Sir EDMUND HILLARY (Ed.): from *Ecology 2000*, (Michael Joseph), by permission of the publishers.

Travel

PAUL THEROUX: from *The Kingdom by the Sea*, (Hamish Hamilton, 1983), by permission of Aitken & Stone, agents. DAPHNE DU MAURIER: from *Vanishing Cornwall*, (Victor Gollancz, 1967), Copyright © 1967 by Daphne du Maurier and Christian Browning, by permission of Christian Browning and Du Maurier Productions, Ltd. JOHN BETJEMAN: RICHARD CAREW: from *Survey of Cornwall*, and D.H. LAWRENCE: from *Letters*, as quoted in A.L. ROWSE (Ed.), *A Cornish Anthology*, (Macmillan, 1968, reissued by Alison Hodge, 1982), by permission of the publishers. ROBERT HUNT: from *Cornish Legends*, (Tor Mark Press), by permission of the publishers. A.D. HIPPISLEY COXE: from *A Book About Smuggling in the West Country*, (Tabb House, 1984), by permission of the publishers. ERIC NEWBY: from *A Short Walk on the Hindu Kush*, (Collins Harvill, 1981), by permission of the publishers.

Talking As Writing

DANNY DANZINGER: from *All In a Day's Work*, (Fontana, 1987), by permission of Collins, publishers. SUE SHARPE (Ed.): from Rosemary's story in *Falling for Love: Teenage Mother's Talk*, (Virago, 1987), Copyright © Sue Sharpe, 1987, by permission of the publishers.

Letters and Diaries

GILBERT WHITE: from *Gilbert White's Year*, (The Scolar Press, 1979), by permission of the publishers. JANET MARSH: from *Nature Diary*, (Michael Joseph, 1979), by permission of the publishers. AIDAN MACFARLANE and ANN McPHERSON, illustrated by JOHN ASTROP; from *The Diary of a Teenage Health Freak*, (O.U.P., 1987), by permission of the publishers.

Miscellaneous

PIERS PAUL READ: from *The Train Robbers*, (W.H. Allen, 1978), by permission of the publishers. SHEILA SULLIVAN: article from *The Guardian* (30 December 1987), by permission of the author and Guardian Newspapers Ltd. Article from *The Independent* (5 March 1987), by permission of Newspaper Publishing plc.

While every effort has been made to obtain permission from copyright holders, this has not been possible in one or two cases. We apologize for any apparent negligence.

The Editor and Publishers thank Sue Wallis for permission to reproduce *First Experiences* (p9). Particular thanks to Brian Keaney (research).